Murder and Mystery on Grand Mesa

A FISHING FEUD BEGINS

James K. Wetzel

James K. Wetzel

LIFETIME CHRONICLE PRESS/dba
LONDON PUBLISHING
Montrose, CO

About the Cover Art

The cover art, "Grand Mesa Revenge," was created by western pencil artist Ron Morris, Sr. of Naturita, Colorado. He has earned the reputation of having the unique ability to capture tremendous depth and feeling in just a moment of time in Western life, making the resulting image special and real. This pencil sketch reflects the torching of the Grand Mesa Hotel as it might have appeared on July 17, 1901, as a lantern is tossed into the open doorway. I am most grateful to Ron for capturing this image of our early history so effectively.

James K. Wetzel

© 2011 James K. Wetzel
All rights reserved in whole or in part.

First edition
Printed in the United States
Library of Congress Control Number: 2010939780
ISBN: 978-0-9822935-7-7

Cover and book design by Laurie Goralka Design

Lifetime Chronicle Press/dba
London Publishing
10614 Bostwick Park Rd.
Montrose, CO 81401
970-240-1153
chronicle@montrose.net
www.londonpublishing.net

Table of Contents

Acknowledgements 5
Introduction 7
CHAPTER 1
  The Western Slope is Settled 10
CHAPTER 2
  William Alexander—A Man of Mystery 14
CHAPTER 3
  Richard Forrest—A Visionary 18
CHAPTER 4
  William Alexander Meets Richard Forrest 21
CHAPTER 5
  Fishing and Irrigation Water on Grand Mesa . . . 27
CHAPTER 6
  William Alexander Disappears 33
CHAPTER 7
  Fishing Law of 1893 38
CHAPTER 8
  Sam Cockreham Sells His Claim 42
CHAPTER 9
  Richard Forrest—New Responsibilities 45
CHAPTER 10
  William Radcliffe Appears 47
CHAPTER 11
  William A. Womack—Cattleman 53
CHAPTER 12
  Radcliffe Makes New Rules 56
CHAPTER 13
  Fishing Laws Change Again in 1899 62
CHAPTER 14
  Radcliffe Makes Improvements to the Resort . . . 68
CHAPTER 15
  Who Was Frank A. Mahany? 71

CHAPTER 16
A Good Day for Fishing 77
CHAPTER 17
Mahany Turns Himself In 82
CHAPTER 18
Mob Heads for the Lakes 86
CHAPTER 19
Radcliffe Was Out of Town. 92
CHAPTER 20
Commissioner Harris Investigates 103
CHAPTER 21
No Protection, Says Governor 105
CHAPTER 22
The Mob Returns to the Mesa 110
CHAPTER 23
Mahany Goes to Prison. 113
CHAPTER 24
Radcliffe Returns to Delta 120
CHAPTER 25
Radcliffe Sues for Damages 123
CHAPTER 26
Radcliffe Settles His Affairs and Goes Home 130
CHAPTER 27
Mahany is Pardoned and Kills Again 135
CHAPTER 28
The Story Continues 140
CHAPTER 29
A Skeleton is Found 143
CHAPTER 30
Alexander Found? 154
CHAPTER 31
Author's Comments Regarding William Alexander . . . 160
End Notes 164
Bibliography 168
Index 171

Acknowledgements

This book has come together with the support and encouragement of many people, and in addition to assistance from many sources within Colorado; other participating contributors from the western states of Oregon, Utah, Idaho, New Mexico, and Minnesota have also provided valuable pieces of this story.

I credit the Delta County Historical Society as the single most valuable resource for solid historical documents and photographs relating to this event of 1901. For 46 years, the DCHS has gathered and contributed material to their museum archive, and that has included the federal and state government documents mentioned in this book, as well as numerous local newspaper resources from the late 1800s and early 1900s.

I am especially grateful for the enormous amount of material relating to the early Colorado fish and game laws provided by Chris Kennedy of the United States Fish and Wildlife Service, and the time and effort he expended providing early newspaper facsimiles from Denver archive resources. Much of that material assisted in clarifying the historical context of some of the events noted herein.

My thanks to Katie Hynes of Gunnison County and Lyndee Dean of Pitkin County for assisting with research of county land records within their home counties, and to Cindy Hines, Executive Director of the Frontier Historical Museum in Glenwood Springs, Colorado, for her assistance with local historical research for this book effort.

Thanks also to Linda Bledsoe of the U.S. Forest Service, Uncompahgre National Forest offices with her vast knowledge of the history of Grand Mesa water resources, and her insight in relating the geography of the mesa to the early history, and to Darrell Munsell, author and historian in Redstone, Colorado, for his knowledge and assistance with the Redstone connection to this story.

And thanks, also, for the gracious contribution of third-generation Richard Forrest descendant, Elizabeth Chaya, and the family history she was willing to provide in support of the Forrest legacy.

Finally, I wish to thank my wife, Nancy, for her encouragement and support of this literary project.

I could not close without paying homage to the pioneers and early settlers of Delta County, whose stories reflect the strength of spirit with which this county was created, and to the writers and historians who have so carefully documented their history.

Introduction

The settlement of the "wild west" has been documented in thousands of stories about our hardy pioneers and their interaction with everything from weather conditions to marauding Indians, outlaws and lawmen, gold and silver, and just about anything else you can imagine in one's search for a better life. The settlement of the Western Slope[1] of Colorado was no exception, because all of the aforementioned elements played a role.

Colorado's Western Slope pioneer history typically began in September of 1881 with the removal of the Ute Indians from their reservation, which encompassed almost the entire Western Slope area. The Consolidated Ute Reservation was formed in 1871 by the United States Congress to protect the seven Ute bands located therein from pioneer incursion into the Ute cultural territory, where they had lived for hundreds of years prior. Unfortunately, a series of incidents, not the least of which was the discovery of vast resources of gold and silver by early prospectors, led to altercations with the Utes—initiated by both Indian and government (U.S. Army Cavalry) elements—such that the nationwide cry, "The Utes Must Go," pervaded. Thus it was that President Benjamin Harrison declared the Ute Reservation dissolved and open for settlement once the majority of the Indians were relocated to Utah.

Colorado's Grand Mesa, sometimes referred to by the Utes as "Thunder Mountain," was a major part of the reservation, offering superior hunting and fishing in over 200 lakes located there. The attraction of the Grand Mesa to our early settlers was for much the same reason, though travel to the mesa was often difficult on the former Indian trails.

History has noted that both Delta and Grand Junction, Colorado, were settled at nearly the same time, thanks to the vision and mission of a man named George A. Crawford. Though the two towns were on opposite sides of the Grand Mesa, both saw the recreational value of such a vast area, and even then referred to the mesa as the "World's Largest Flat-top Mountain." Though skiing and other winter sports came later, "recreation" in this sense referred to fishing and hunting, then a source of food for hungry families trying to make a living farming or ranching on the fertile lands below. The recreational development of the Grand Mesa also had its historical moments, the most famous of which I have documented in this book.

Writing a book, regardless of the subject, speaks to some form of motivation by the writer, and this book is no different. When the subject is about a murder, albeit not an unsolved one, the topic jumps a notch or two in interest. This murder, often described by historians as the story of the Grand Mesa Feud, has carried that title in numerous newspapers and magazines and book chapters for over a hundred years.

Some have written that the feud, in various forms, lasted over 50 years and involved something as simple as fishing in what most believed were public waters, for our early pioneers fished and hunted for survival, and no one thought any different...that is, until fish and game laws permitted private ownership of lakes and reservoirs on public land, even in the 1890s.

This book is not intended to carry the 50-year story. The focus is on the killing of a Cedaredge cattleman, the events that led up to it, and some details of events that followed. A second story deals with the disappearance of a key player early in the first story, which has yet to be definitively solved.

While researching this story might have appeared to be easy due to the numerous newspaper articles and other write-ups about the event, I was astounded to discover the misinformation that has been carried forward by so many writers, whether they be historians or simply reporters. My wish, when you read this story, is that the reader will see the events in a slightly different light than that presented elsewhere.

This story included international ramifications with England, presidential oversight by two U.S. presidents (Theodore Roosevelt and William Taft), and action by the United States Congress, all over the murder of a local cattleman from Eckert, Colorado, who simply wanted to go fishing on a Sunday after-

Introduction

noon on the Grand Mesa with several of his cowboys, all who had earned a well-deserved break from working on a ditch system that carried much-needed irrigation water to crops below. Even before William A. Womack was brutally murdered in front of five witnesses, numerous prior incidents foretold the possibility of events that might culminate in serious injury or even death.

Ten years before the Womack killing, another mystery regarding the same Grand Mesa resort area was publicized when former owner and partner, William Alexander, disappeared mysteriously on a trip to Delta and was never seen again in Delta County. This puzzle will also be explored, where new evidence has been discovered that may explain the why and where of Alexander's disappearance.

The incident on the Grand Mesa spanned a period of about 25 years, beginning with the incorporation of the Surface Creek Ditch and Reservoir Company in 1886; the preemption[2] of 160 acres of forest land and fishing lakes by William Alexander in 1888; and ending with final restitution to William Radcliffe in 1909, in payment of damages for the loss of his home and resort by mob rule and arson in 1901.

Because the timeline of these events is rather complex, I have chosen to tell them chronologically, with occasional side trips to bring other facts and details into the story. My writing style is to present verified facts in such a way that they tell the story, and not to make up missing details to make it all sound good. As any other historian and author will confess, there comes a time when one feels that enough information is on hand to tell the story, even though other facts may be discovered down the road to add to it. Thus, this book represents that point for me.

The main characters of my book are more than just names, thus I have attempted to tell a little about their lives, as well. In doing so, I have looked at what happened to these people with a new perspective. Readers familiar with the events herein are invited to seek their own perspectives. Enjoy!

CHAPTER 1

The Western Slope is Settled

A treaty with the Ute Indians in 1868 created the Consolidated Ute Reservation, which enclosed most of the Western Slope of Colorado: from Gunnison, south through Pagosa Springs to the New Mexico border, west to the Utah border, north to about the Rangely area, east to the Yampa River, and south following a line through present-day Aspen to Gunnison, forming a rough rectangle. The eastern edge of the reservation was just west of the present-day town of Gunnison, though in 1868, Gunnison did not exist, the settlement starting about 1874. While the reservation was intended to prohibit the movement of our early pioneers into reservation territory, the discovery of gold and silver deposits in the San Juan Mountains and other areas by miners who broke the rules could not stop a steady influx of those seeking to get rich. In fact, miners were in the area even before the treaty was signed in 1868, as gold was discovered in the San Juans about 1860, at a time when travel in the area by the pioneers was not restricted but often dangerous due to the bands of Utes that roamed the Western Slope.

When Chief Ouray of the Utes requested that the United States government increase their presence in the area of the San Juans to remove the miners from the reservation, the miners made it clear that any attempt to do so would be met with guns and force. The government, rather than spill the blood of the miners, chose instead to remove the San Juan Mountains from the reservation. Problem solved! The treaty of 1873 eliminated almost 540 square miles of Ute territory with the stroke of a pen, nearly one-fourth of the reservation. The government, according to the terms of this treaty, was also supposed to include $500,000

CHAPTER 1: The Western Slope is Settled

in annuities to the Utes, often paid in the form of cattle, sheep, tools, housing, or combinations of these. Most was never paid.

The Utes were not happy with the outcome of the Brunot Treaty (or Agreement) of 1873, named for the chief United States government negotiator, Philip Brunot. Since Congress had abolished Indian sovereignty and treaty rights in 1871, the Indians were not able to negotiate agreements from a place of strength.

Colorado became a state on July 4, 1876. In the years prior to this, Colorado was a territory consisting of 17 counties, 16 of them on the Front Range (east of the Continental Divide) and one large county, called "Lake County," on the Western Slope. In 1875, even though most of the Western Slope of Colorado was a single county, much of the territory consisted of the Consolidated Ute Reservation. The county seat was in Leadville.

It didn't help the Indian position when the Little Bighorn massacre of General George Armstrong Custer and his battalion took place less than two weeks before Colorado statehood. There was a clamor at the time to remove all Indians in the West, with public sentiment against them at an all-time high.

With Colorado statehood, the state legislature acted immediately to split Lake County, and Gunnison County was created in 1877, an area slightly larger than the state of Massachusetts. It included the area later encompassed by Gunnison, Montrose, Delta, and Mesa Counties.

When Indian Agent Nathan C. Meeker of the White River Agency to the north was massacred by the Northern Utes along with nine of his employees in September 1879, Colorado became the focus of the popular editorial of the day: "The Utes Must Go." Little more than three years had elapsed since the Custer massacre, and there was renewed interest in Congress to do something about the "Indian problem."

In Colorado, a new agreement was "negotiated" between the Utes and the United States government. This agreement, signed by Chief Ouray and nine Ute tribal leaders on March 6, 1880, effectively closed the Consolidated Ute Reservation, moved the Northern Ute tribes into Utah to an expanded Uintah Reservation, and sent the Southern Ute tribes to a new reservation at Ignacio, Colorado. Thus, by presidential decree, President

MURDER AND MYSTERY ON GRAND MESA

William Harrison ordered the Utes to vacate their reservation in late August 1881 under U.S. Army Cavalry escort, and the area was open for settlement on September 3, 1881.

For the next year and a half, Gunnison County grew rapidly with the creation of larger towns such as Grand Junction, Uncompahgre (officially changed to "Delta" on August 31, 1882), and Montrose, along with many smaller towns. The town of Gunnison, then the county seat, was thriving, as it was the jumping-off point for settlers heading further west and north on the Western Slope. A mining rush had occurred in 1879, the spillover from the Leadville discoveries. Enough gold was found to cause a boom, and 1880 found men flocking into the county. The Denver & Rio Grande railroad had reached Gunnison in 1877, but there it stopped, because it could not penetrate the Ute Reservation still in place beyond the town. When the reservation was disbanded in 1881, the railroad was quick to continue on to Montrose, then expanded north to Delta and Grand Junction by November 1882.

Word got around after the Meeker Massacre and the treaty of 1880 that the Utes would be leaving, and a number of curious settlers—usually in large, well-armed groups of 10 to 15 men—snuck into the reservation early to check out the resources such as the availability of good farmland and grass for cattle, and no doubt some were exploring for precious metals. These were short excursions, as the cavalry, stationed at Fort Crawford just south of soon-to-be Montrose, was on the lookout for illegal settlers and those caught were sometimes placed in the brig at the fort. Because of the Meeker incident, the army beefed up its manpower and other resources at Fort Crawford and also built a wagon road up to Grand Mesa, generally following existing Indian trails. An army encampment was also built at Military Park (as it was later named) because of a fear of a Ute uprising following the 1880 Ute Agreement. Though short lived, the soldiers camped on Grand Mesa had ample time to discover the many lakes there as well as the abundance of fish and game nearby. This information spread rapidly among military and civilian residents alike.

It was in this environment that word certainly got back to Gunnison regarding the tremendous opportunities to claim, under the Homestead Act, rich farmland for a new life in the

CHAPTER 1: The Western Slope is Settled

West. Westward expansion was in full swing, and this was virgin territory to settle and start a new life. People such as Richard Forrest and William Alexander, principal characters in this story, and thousands more were probably avid listeners to any written or spoken word regarding the fine land beyond Gunnison, and it drew them as a bear is drawn to honey.

Gunnison, as a hub, became the supply center. Great freight wagons drawn by four- and eight-horse teams lumbered over roads that were little better than trails. In places there were toll roads with tolls scaled to fit the occasion, thanks to Otto Mears and his associates. Towns mushroomed wherever the need arose. In the history of Gunnison County, there have been more than a hundred towns, most of which are now "ghosts."

It didn't take long for the Gunnison representatives to the Colorado legislature to realize that natural obstacles such as the Gunnison River, the Uncompahgre River, and the Black Canyon created significant travel difficulties within the county, especially when elections meant that ballots had to be carried by horseback, sometimes over a hundred miles, back to Gunnison. So, on February 11, 1883, the Colorado legislature divided Gunnison County into four smaller counties—Gunnison, Montrose, Delta, and Mesa. By doing so, legal matters—from filing claims, recording other documents, and handling elections—could be taken care of easier and quicker.

The stage was set for the four new counties to define their own distinct futures. In less than a month after becoming a county, Delta had her first newspaper, *The Delta Chief.* The *Chief* still exists today, having undergone several name changes over the years, but nevertheless, Delta now had a means of advertising her abundance, and advertise she did! Newspapers found their way to the East Coast and points in-between, and pioneer settlers began to filter in—from Pennsylvania, Missouri, Kentucky, Ohio, New Jersey, New York, and just about every other state. The players in this little melodrama began to assemble, and William Radcliffe, an Englishman, came all the way from London to play a key role in events that would unfold during the 1890s and early 1900s in Delta County, Colorado.

CHAPTER 2

William Alexander—
A Man of Mystery

One of those early settlers was a man named William Alexander. It is believed that Alexander came to Delta County, Colorado, in early 1886. There is no evidence as to where he came from or anything about him. He was apparently a very private man and rarely disclosed any details of his life prior to coming to Delta County. There is no record of where Alexander lived his first two years here, but since he made no preemption claim until 1888, he probably resided in a hand-built cabin on Grand Mesa on the land he was to subsequently preempt.

We do know that William Alexander was one of the original directors of the Surface Creek Ditch and Reservoir Company, incorporated in October 1886. His signature, the only ever uncovered by his hand, appears on the incorporation document. And since he was working for the Surface Creek Ditch and Reservoir Company, their efforts were focused on the mesa.

We also know that William Alexander brought with him a registered stock brand, suggesting some prior involvement in the cattle business. He sold the brand on April 13, 1889, to Charles Campbell of Delta for $5. Campbell was only 18 years old at the time, and single. The brand was two initials, "R.A.," and somewhat puzzling as to what the R might have stood for. If the A stood for Alexander, what did the R mean? This brand was registered as a state brand.[3]

The Surface Creek Ditch and Reservoir Company was formed to improve the irrigation resources for the Surface Creek Valley, and their plan was to build dams on many of the lakes on Grand Mesa to raise the water level in the lake by 10 feet or more. In this manner, many additional acre-feet of water could

CHAPTER 2: William Alexander—A Man of Mystery

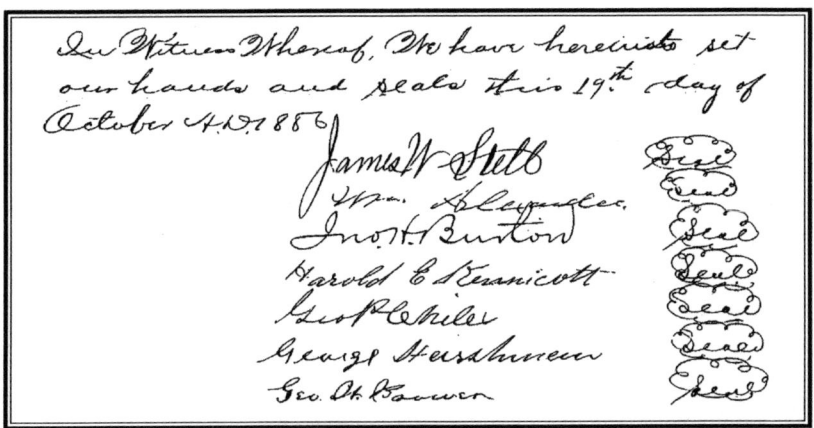

Signatures on the incorporation document for the Surface Creek Ditch and Reservoir Company. William Alexander's signature is second from the top.
Credit: Delta County Clerk and Recorder Office

be stored for release to the farms below. In addition to the dams, ditches were built to connect various lakes, and other diversion ditches were built to initially direct the water to Ward and Kiser Creeks, then to Surface Creek and beyond. Lakes were acquired by filing legal documents for the water, and by 1900, SCD&RC had filed on 21 lakes or reservoirs on Grand Mesa.

The first public mention of William Alexander was a short statement in *The Delta Independent* newspaper of September 1888, noting that he was employed on the Surface Creek Ditch and Reservoir Company's new ditch, that he had just preempted 160 acres of land on the Grand Mesa, and that he was planning to go into the fish business, as his land included three lakes that he planned to stock with trout and carp. The three lakes, unnamed at the time, were soon referred to as "Alexander Lake" and the "Twin Lakes," and collectively referred to as the Alexander Group of lakes. Alexander, himself, referred to "his" lake originally as "Fish Lake" and the rest of the area as his Fish Lake Resort.

Alexander probably checked out other nearby lakes on the mesa and noted that most of the lakes contained native trout. Some appeared to contain lots of fish, some very few fish, and some, no fish at all. Barren Lake got its name for the latter reason.

The newspaper article further stated that Alexander planned to live on his place all winter. There is no evidence that he didn't live on his land, but if this was his first winter on the mesa, he must have had some anxious moments with the harsh elements and sheer logistics of survival. Though it was never mentioned, he most likely had built a cabin a few years earlier and was already familiar with the cold and snowy winters.

Spring came late on Grand Mesa, simply because the winter snowfall usually amounted to 16 to 20 feet, and that amount of snow would take a while to melt. Also, because his lakes were close to the 10,000-foot elevation of the mesa, ice would remain on them a bit longer. The ice, however, was to be an asset to his planned fish business, for it would later be used to pack his fresh mountain trout in for delivery to local and distant markets.

Thus, in the spring of 1889, Alexander began to improve his land further by building a fish hatchery on the north shore of Alexander Lake—the beginning of his dream to start a fish business. In March 1889, William Alexander announced that his Fish Lake Resort would be open in the late spring. It is presumed that Alexander had no buildings yet, other than his residence, since he had only moved onto his land the previous fall. At that time, the "resort" consisted of nothing more than a campground, if that, and permission to fish in the lakes on his property.

By August of 1889, when Alexander came to town (Delta) to purchase some provisions, he announced that he was feeding and taking care of about 30 pleasure seekers at that time at his Fish Lake Resort. It is likely that he provided meals for them during their outing to the mesa. In those days, a journey to Grand Mesa from Delta was usually an all-day affair by carriage or wagon, faster by horse, but, nevertheless, one would not plan a round-trip in one day. And certainly, time for fishing had to be factored in.

For many, fishing in those days was more for survival than for sport. It was not uncommon, even occasionally on Alexander's lakes, to hear the sound of dynamite exploding underwater as a means of securing a large catch for family meals for the future. Though illegal, even in those times, fish and game laws were very clear on the acceptable means of fishing. The use of dynamite was not common, as most people also saw the sport in fishing with line and hook.[4] There was no law limiting the number of

CHAPTER 2: William Alexander—A Man of Mystery

fish one could catch, but it was clear on the acceptable methods of catching them.

There is no record that Alexander—or later, when he had a partner—ever charged a fee to fish in his lakes. The public simply would not have paid to fish, nor did Alexander have the resources or the authority to police such a rule on his lakes. Later, when he had a few handmade boats, he probably charged a rental fee for their use.

Since Alexander was in the fish business, it would later become clear how he was able to catch so many fish the first year. Like most of his resort guests, he was not out on his lake with line and hook, catching one fish at a time. Many stories originating from the fishing lakes in those days referred to fishing by seine—using a net to gather the fish.

The small fish hatchery was not expected to supply trout for eating, but to hatch eggs and to grow the fingerlings for stocking other lakes owned by the Surface Creek Ditch and Reservoir Company. Alexander had no agreement with the state Fish and Game Commission to supply eggs for other lakes or reservoirs; that would come later under William Radcliffe's ownership of the business.

It would not be long before William Alexander was to take on a partner, a man who did not necessarily share his vision of raising and selling fish, but who had the resources to finance a fancy hotel on the mesa and share in the financial rewards of the resort operation. The partnership, however, was destined to be a short one.

CHAPTER 3

Richard Forrest— A Visionary

Alexander's soon-to-be partner, Richard Forrest, had immigrated from County Cork, Ireland, at the age of 21. He came from a large family that likely had very little land or money. So as soon as each child was old enough, they left home for other parts of the world. When Forrest came of age, he said good-by to his family and took a ship to America, landing in Boston in 1866. Forrest was known to be a horse lover, and soon after his arrival in Boston, he took a job as coachman for a very wealthy man. He remained in Boston at his job for about seven years and, hearing many stories about how the West was being opened up for settlement, he finally moved on to Missouri and bought some land and teams of mules. He liked Missouri but suffered from attacks of what was then called "ague" but is now known as malaria.

While in Missouri, family records revealed that he had occasion to meet outlaw Jesse James, though no one knows how well he knew him. Whenever James and his sordid past came up for discussion, Forrest would end the conversation by saying, "Well, no matter what he did, he was always good to his mother!" I guess he felt that was sufficient excuse for any bad deed.

Forrest remained in Missouri for another seven years, then headed further west to Denver, taking his teams and wagons, and probably some helpers, with him. At that time, western Colorado was still an Indian reservation for the Ute tribes. In Denver, Forrest established a freight line between Denver and Cripple Creek, then a booming mining community. He transported food and other supplies needed by the miners and brought back ore from the mines for processing.

CHAPTER 3: Richard Forrest—A Visionary

Perhaps his contact with miners got into his blood, for in 1880, we find him in Gunnison County, working as a miner in Ruby City, today a ghost town outside the town of Gunnison. Mining never was big in the Gunnison region because the ore was considered poor grade and thus did not attract many looking for quick riches. By 1883, mining had all but played out, and most of those searching for precious metals had moved on to other areas.

The narrow gauge railroad made it to Gunnison in 1877 but could go no further west because the Ute reservation started just west of Gunnison, and as long as the reservation was there, the railroad would not penetrate Ute land. That all changed when the reservation was dissolved in September 1881, allowing the railroad to push on to Montrose and beyond. Gunnison became a storage and staging area for a few years, and was a jumping-off point for many settlers heading for the Western Slope of Colorado, once the area was open for settlement.

While the potential riches offered by mining drew Richard Forrest to the Western Slope, it was his cousin, William, that drew him to Delta County. William, too, had lived in the Gunnison area, arriving there in 1881. While it is not certain what he did there, it is assumed that he was either a miner or worked with the mines, as not too many years later, he worked as an assayer for the mines in Ouray and Telluride. William worked in Gunnison for two years and came to Delta County shortly after the county was formed in 1883. Something drew him to the Surface Creek Valley, where he soon met a local girl, Sarah A. Weir, who had moved with her parents and siblings to the Eckert area in 1883. A courtship developed, and William and Sarah were married on December 14, 1884. Perhaps, as cousins, William and Richard had met and worked together or lived in Gunnison at the same time, or maybe they had communicated by letter. Whichever was the case, William, no doubt, extolled on the virtues of the area he had settled in Eckert, Colorado, for Richard was to follow within a year.

Following the removal of the Indians in late 1881, Richard Forrest knew that the area was virgin territory for new settlement. So, following his unsuccessful mining experience, he finally made the move to Delta County in 1884 and lived with

William and Sarah for a short while before staking a preemptive claim on 169 acres in the Eckert area, then still not much more than a wide space in the road.

Forrest built a home and began farming his land almost immediately. For several years, he grew mostly wheat, oats, alfalfa, and potatoes, the latter a fondness acquired from his Irish roots. He planted an orchard of one acre, and within 10 years, had close to 40 acres of fruit. While he had a love of horses, he owned only two horses and two mules; the horses were for transportation, and the mules were probably for farm work. He also had just over 100 acres of irrigated land. Located just north of today's Fruitgrowers Reservoir, his land made up the lower end of Harts Basin and is even today considered some of the best farmland in the county.

Did William Alexander pass by this farm in his travels back and forth from Grand Mesa? He most certainly passed nearby, as the main trail and wagon road to the mesa was not far away. Though not heavily traveled, it was the main horse and wagon road between the mesa and valley roads. It was originally an Indian trail and had been improved by the U.S. Army Cavalry shortly after the Utes were removed from the area in late 1881.

It was in this setting that Richard Forrest's life was to begin a new chapter.

CHAPTER 4
William Alexander Meets Richard Forrest

No one knows exactly how William Alexander and Richard Forrest met. What is known is that William Alexander is the one who had the idea of creating a fishing resort on Grand Mesa, as he was the one who preempted and settled on the land.

Both men were single, with Forrest about age 40 and Alexander a few years younger. Forrest was a lonely man, and whenever he heard a horse, wagon, or carriage on the road near his home, it was both from curiosity and generosity that he would greet the occupant(s) and invite the person(s) in for a meal or overnight accommodation. It may have been from such an encounter that he first met William Alexander, as Alexander often rode to Delta for provisions or to deliver fish to the train depot for shipment.

The partnership between Alexander and Forrest may have solidified as early as February 1890, when *The Delta Independent* newspaper reported: "Richard Forrest has fitted up a first class resort on the Grand mesa, about twenty-five miles from Delta. This will be a grand thing for those wishing to spend a few days on the Grand mesa."

This was the first appearance of Forrest's name in connection with the resort on Grand Mesa. He had no property there, so the newspaper reference was probably connected to Alexander's resort.

In a June 1890 issue of *The Delta Independent*, it was reported that: "Wm. Alexander was in town yesterday from his fish hatchery on Grand Mesa. He has four men busily at work fixing up ponds, screens, ditches, etc., and hopes to have some fish in the market soon - reg'lar trout." With this small snippet from the newspaper, we can conclude that the Alexander-Forrest fish hatchery on Grand Mesa was started in early 1890.

At about this same time, Alexander and Forrest formed a partnership for the resort and fishing project. In July 1890, Alexander shipped his first load of trout to mountain towns nearby. But it wasn't until the next year, about the same time as the grand opening of the hotel, that Alexander and Forrest decided to legalize the partnership, and an agreement was executed on November 6, 1891. The agreement stated that the purpose of the partnership was to form stock-raising, contracting, and fish culture, and called for the joint ownership—or an undivided half interest—of both the Forrest holdings of 169 acres in Eckert and the Alexander property of 162 acres on Grand Mesa, as well as the hotel and resort operation. It also specified that Alexander was to pay Forrest $2,500 in consideration. Perhaps the "consideration" was half the cost of the hotel that Forrest had financed or to remedy the imbalance of the joint contributions. But the agreement clearly stated that "such amount shall be paid to the said Forrest out of the said partnership property before anything shall be paid to the said Alexander..."

It is likely that it was Richard Forrest who proposed to build the hotel for the resort operation. Years later, he disclosed that he was the financier of the resort project and supposedly a silent partner while Alexander was the front man, operating the resort and actually living there, as well. In reality, Forrest was never exactly "silent" regarding his role in the project.

In mid-summer of 1890, Alexander and Forrest began the construction of a new hotel on Grand Mesa, and at the same time, Alexander attached his name to the lake where the hotel was to be built. While the name "Alexander Lake" has remained ever since, the hotel underwent several name changes throughout its short 10-year history.

The Alexander Hotel was built under contract with Gale Brothers, a builder based in the town of Delta. This would not have been a job where the workmen would go home at the end of the work day. Several cabins were built first for the workmen, so that they would not have to travel home during the week. The completed hotel was two stories high, had nine bedrooms—four upstairs and five on the main floor—a kitchen, hall, and dining

CHAPTER 4: William Alexander Meets Richard Forrest

and sitting rooms. A large covered porch in front, on both levels, provided an area for sitting and relaxation. It was a log structure throughout and was considered to be, in those times, a first-class resort.

A Grand Junction newspaper reported that the Mesa Lakes Resort[5] was "without any doubt the finest natural resort in the state." It had a hotel, several cabins and tents available, and also boasted of having "frequent catches of trout weighing two pounds or more."

The Alexander Hotel officially opened for business in late July 1891. It was strictly a summer business, as winter snows made travel on the mesa almost impossible, and the hotel was, of course, not heated, either. A popular event at the hotel was to take visitors on picnics to various parts of the Alexander property, which probably also included some fishing. The operation of the Alexander resort, along with the sale of fish, continued to be profitable by most standards, at least through July 1891, but about the time that the hotel opened for business, the sale of fish hit a snag—a big one.

The earliest photo of Alexander Hotel, probably taken at or near completion of the construction of the hotel, about June 1891. The central figure with white shirt, vest, and hand on hip is Richard Forrest. The figure upstairs with the lady by his side is possibly William Alexander, though there are no other pictures of him for comparison.
Photo credit: Ellen Bond (a descendant of the photographer, Francis M. Laycook)

MURDER AND MYSTERY ON GRAND MESA

In late June 1891, the *Leadville Daily* and *Evening Chronicle* reported that a shipment of 200 pounds of trout had been brought to Leadville[6] and sold to a wholesale dealer, who in turn retailed them out in small lots. The matter was brought to the attention of Deputy Fish Commissioner Land, whose office was in Leadville. The problem with such a sale was that the fish laws at the time prohibited the capture and indiscriminate slaughter of fish obtained from *public waters* and sold in this manner. An investigation by Fish Commissioner Land at Alexander Lake showed that Alexander was trapping mature trout from adjacent streams and moving them to a holding area at the lake for later sale. The adjacent streams were public waters, thus it was a violation of state fish laws to trap them.

Some thought Alexander was seining fish traveling upstream in public waters to spawn in the spring, while others told of Alexander closing the headgate at the Alexander Lake dam, whereby the public waters stream, now void of water below the headgate, would reveal fish flopping around in the mud, and he would collect them, place them in a tank of sorts, and deposit them in his holding pond for later sale. This took at least two men to work the process, since the stream could not be void of water for very long, else their act would be readily discovered. There were other illegal techniques as well, but the key point was that once the fish were on the other side of the dam headgate, they were in public waters.

Not only was the person who caught and wholesaled the fish breaking the law, but any merchant selling the fish was also breaking the law. Upon investigation, the Deputy Fish Commissioner determined that the fish had come from public waters below Alexander Lake on the Grand Mesa, and Alexander was shipping them to Leadville and Ouray merchants. So, in mid-July, Alexander was arrested, tried, and subsequently fined for breaking the law, along with three merchants in Leadville and several in Ouray. Each was fined $50 and court costs. Alexander and the others were reported to have paid their fines.

It is hard to imagine that both Alexander and Forrest were not aware of the law, but if they were, it is not likely that Alexander would have brought the fish to Leadville with the Deputy Fish Commissioner not far away. What is interesting about this

CHAPTER 4: William Alexander Meets Richard Forrest

incident is that it never was made public in Delta County and never appeared in Delta's local newspaper.

Now that both Alexander and Forrest were under scrutiny by the Fish Commissioner, the plan to sell fish from their lakes at that time was brought to a halt. Not being able to sell fish did not interfere with the imminent opening of the resort and hotel. It may have been this incident that encouraged them to focus more on the small fish hatchery near the shore of Alexander Lake, though when Fish Commissioner Land actually visited the resort immediately after the Leadville incident, he remarked, "No hatchery was on the place nor ever had been." If there was no hatchery, why did Alexander claim there was one earlier in 1890? We do know from photos of the Alexander hatchery that it was not a permanent structure. It was set up in the spring before spawning and probably taken down before winter. Perhaps by July of 1891, it had already been taken down or was never set up that year at all.

Did this entire incident affect Alexander's long-term plans, and perhaps give him the motivation to bail on the entire scheme and look elsewhere for his pot of gold?

Another factor might have come into play here. In 1891, Leadville was a booming mining community. Three railroads served the town and mining area, and by 1893, the population had grown to 60,000. The Leadville National Fish Hatchery was built in 1889, resulting in the presence of state fish and game employees in the area. Alexander was not oblivious to the tremendous market for fish in Leadville, nor was he blind to the riches being removed from Leadville, as there was a silver boom at the time. Perhaps he was beginning to realize that there was more money to be gained beneath the soil rather than beneath the water.

In spite of the fish business setback, there were plenty of visitors to Alexander Lake in those early years. One entrepreneur—a man named Bert Stroud, living in the town of De Beque on the north side of Grand Mesa—offered tourists, for a fee of $5, travel by train from the Grand Junction depot to De Beque, and from there by saddle horse to either the Mesa Lakes area (on the north side of the mesa) or the Alexander Lakes and Hotel (on the south side of Grand Mesa), and then a return trip.

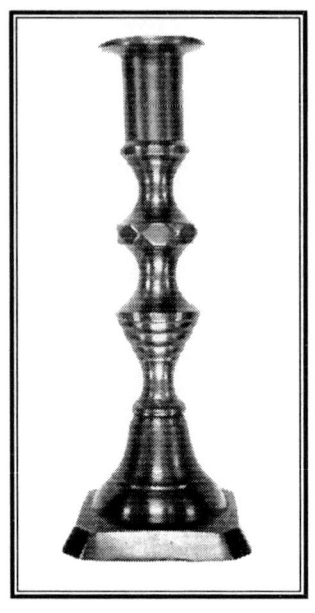

Candlestick. This eight-inch brass candlestick was used in the original Alexander and Forrest hotels. When Richard Forrest sold the hotel in 1896, this candlestick, and perhaps others, was kept by his family. It is now on exhibit at the Delta County Museum.
Photo credit: Delta County Historical Society

He started this service for tourists in early July 1892 and ran such excursions every Tuesday, Thursday, and Saturday, leaving Grand Junction by train at eight o'clock in the morning, and arriving for lunch about two in the afternoon. On his very first such excursion, he had 22 passengers. With comfortable hotels and decent food at both destinations, visitors would typically remain for two nights and return on the evening train the third day.

It would seem that the resort envisioned by Alexander and Forrest was finally beginning to really catch on with the public, on both sides of the Grand Mesa. However, the Alexander-Forrest resort served primarily the south side of the mesa—the Delta County side—and while fishing was popular both for sport and food, it was the lakes on that side that were important to the resort operation, and that, along with new fishing laws, would lead to unimagined problems for the future of the resort.

CHAPTER 5

Fishing and Irrigation Water on Grand Mesa

When Colorado was admitted to the Union in 1876, the word "conservation," or the use of the word in its modern context, apparently did not exist. It was a time when there was plenty of everything, or at least that was the pervading perception. In spite of this, the territorial assemblies recognized the fact that nature readily supplied game, fowl, and fish for augmenting the domestic food supply, and were aware of the fact that protection and preservation of fish and wildlife was a public necessity. Even before Colorado statehood, the Colorado territorial government enacted a law on November 6, 1861, for the "protection of Trout Fish," prohibiting the use of seine, net, basket, or trap to take fish. A fine between $25 and $50 per day/offense was split between the "complaining witness" and the county treasury where the offense occurred.

Existing law was appended in 1872 to include the prohibition of the use of explosives, poison, and stupefying drugs, and stated further that fishing was only legal with hook and line. By 1874, the territorial government also extended the law to prohibit fishing in private lakes, ponds, or streams, except by the consent of the proprietor (owner) of said lakes, ponds, or streams.

Early day endeavors to protect game and fish preceded the creation of a department of game and fish, and the first law passed in 1877 following statehood provided for the "protection, preservation and propagation of fish"[7] and made it unlawful to possess or sell fish during November through March. The position of Fish Commissioner[8] was also established. The early laws dealt predominantly with fish, but big game was protected to the extent that the season was closed from January 1 to September 1 each year.

However, game could be killed for food at any time. There were no wardens to enforce the above laws and hunting licenses were not required.

It wasn't until 1887 when fishing laws finally included a limit on quantity, such that one "could only take trout or food fish for food for immediate use, governed in amount and quantity by the reasonable necessities of the person(s) catching such fish." Then in 1889, this provision was extended to include a size limit—six inches or larger—on retained fish.

An attempt was made in the 1887 law to introduce an enforcement provision, whereby each county, through their county commissioners, could appoint up to six fish wardens who would serve without pay. Fishing laws were one thing, enforcement of them quite another! This provision apparently was seldom used, if at all, for it did not appear in the subsequent law of 1889 or later.

The fishing season was shortened in 1893, prohibiting fishing from November through May and allowing only a five-month season, which was expected to begin about the time when spawning was completed.

Finally, in 1897, while retaining the "consumption for immediate use" provision, the legislature added that one could not take more than 20 pounds of fish per day per person. This was the law that was in effect until a huge change was enacted in 1899, one that was to have major repercussions on Grand Mesa.

From day one, Delta and Mesa County pioneers saw the value in the enormous amount of water on Grand Mesa. Even the earliest of surveys counted well over 250 separate bodies of water. The earliest visionaries saw them as potential resources for irrigation water—in the Surface Creek Valley on the Delta County (south) side of the mesa as well as the Grand Valley on the Mesa County (north) side, and in other areas of both counties below the mesa—while others saw the lakes as a source for food. But not all of the lakes or ponds had fish, as some simply dried up in drought years, lacking any ground water sources to keep them filled with water.

The only way to create a water-storage reservoir from an existing lake was to raise the level of the lake, and this could only be done by building a dam at its outlet, the place where

CHAPTER 5: Fishing and Irrigation Water on Grand Mesa

the water flowed into a stream heading downhill. Headgates were placed at or just above the original level of the lake, followed by an earthen dam[9] to raise the water level over time. Some of the lake levels were raised 10 to 20 feet or more, allowing an enormous amount of water to be stored for use during the growing season. Reservoirs could be drained to the level of the headgate, but the lake remained at its original level, or was adjusted as a result of weather factors when the stored water was depleted.

Early surveys showed which lakes and reservoirs could be linked by connecting ditches, and the five major creeks or streams flowing off the mesa in the Surface Creek Valley[10] were deemed the best sources to carry irrigation water to the ranchers and farmers below. Ward Creek, Kiser Creek, Tongue Creek, Young's Creek, and Surface Creek were the names attached to these early sources, while lateral diversion ditches were usually named after their creators or were given other names determined by the stockholders.

Irrigation companies acquired source water by filing claims on the lakes they determined would feed the creeks and streams to carry the water to their users in the valley. Simply filing on the lakes was not enough: They had to connect the lakes with ditches in order to get the water down the mountain. Stockholders in the ditch company either paid cash for shares or worked for them, and it is likely that most of the early shares were the result of sweat equity. Alexander and Forrest were probably such shareholders. A lake or reservoir could not be filed on without a need for the water, i.e., there had to be stockholders who were willing to pay for water diversion to their pastures and farms.

The Surface Creek Ditch and Reservoir Company incorporated in October 1886, issuing 300 shares at a cost of $10 per share, fully capitalized at $3,000. There were seven original stockholders who formed the company, and William Alexander was one of them. All seven became directors that first year of business. This was a curious fact, because no records have surfaced relative to Alexander's need for irrigation water, or exactly where he was living during the two years prior to his preemption claim on the mesa, though it is likely he lived on the mesa in the area he eventually claimed.

The Articles of Incorporation of the Surface Creek Ditch and Reservoir Company stated the following:

> *The object for which our said company is formed and incorporated are to:*
> - Construct, maintain, and operate a ditch or canal for conveying water for domestic purposes and irrigation for use upon the lands of the stockholders of this company only in the county of Delta and State of Colorado, and
> - To construct, maintain and operate lateral or branch irrigating ditches from said main ditch of this company to such localities as will enable our company to use or dispose of the water conducted through its main line for the purposes hereinbefore set forth, and
> - To construct and maintain reservoirs for the purpose of storing water to be conveyed in the said ditches and laterals and for the uses and purposes aforesaid.
> - To acquire, hold and use such premises along the line of our said ditch as may be necessary to the right of way therefore or in the construction or maintenance thereof of laterals.

The Articles went on to describe the manner in which water was to be conveyed and the line of the main ditch, etc. Though the articles made no mention of fishing rights, it is presumed that exclusive fishing rights for SCD&RC stockholders were added in subsequent bylaws, as it was this legal issue that was to culminate in the killing of William A. Womack in 1901.

When Alexander preempted 162 acres on the mesa two years later (1888), his claim included three of the 13 lakes controlled by the SCD&RC at the time. All SCD&RC stockholders had fishing rights in the 13 lakes they controlled, a fact that was to set in motion the 1901 tragedy.

Of course, reservoirs had to be created first, and Alexander probably had his sights set on Alexander Lake and Twin Lakes[11] when he filed his preemption claim in 1888, two years after the ditch company was formed. At first, the lakes and reservoirs were simply numbered—they had no names. Today, reservoir numbers are often still used by the Forest Service and the

CHAPTER 5: Fishing and Irrigation Water on Grand Mesa

Grand Mesa Water Users,[12] even though names are assigned to them. Reservoirs and lakes on Grand Mesa were usually named after the local pioneers who owned part or all of the shoreline. Over time, some of the lakes have had several names, and those details sometimes create confusion as to which lake is being addressed. In this book, original reservoir and lake names have been used. Current names, when different, will be noted in footnotes.

Some other curious facts have been discovered in regard to the Surface Creek Ditch and Reservoir Company. Stock records show that Stock Certificate #1 was issued on August 3, 1894. SCD&RC records also contain just three stock certificates of a previous issue—the earliest dated 1893—which suggest there were earlier stockholders, but without the certificates or certificate stubs that are customarily retained by the company for their records, it is impossible to determine or confirm that William Alexander, Richard Forrest, and William Womack were all early stockholders, as most early write-ups of the "Grand Mesa Feud" story claimed. This writer shall trust that that information is correct. It was also claimed that William A. Womack was one of the largest stockholders.

Richard Forrest also owned 20 stock shares purchased August 9, 1897, and sold in February 1900, after he had sold the Grand Mesa resort. However, in March 1892, Alexander and Forrest executed a 99-year lease with the SCD&RC, where they surrendered their earned irrigation rights of the lakes and in return acquired fish culture rights and fishing privileges in all waters then or afterward controlled during the time of the lease by SCD&RC, retaining to stockholders fishing rights according to law.

The earliest SCD&RC corporate bylaws on file with Grand Mesa Water Users were amended in 1952, thus there is no evidence to verify stockholder fishing rights in SCD&RC lakes or the 99-year lease obtained by Alexander and Forrest. Such facts can only be assumed to be historically accurate, as they were repeatedly mentioned in newspaper articles after the murder in 1901.

The stock shares that were earned or purchased between incorporation in October 1886 and August 1894 were not recorded or retained (except for three), as no records have survived. It could easily have taken eight years to complete the work on the 13 reservoirs under SCD&RC control, and such work had to be done before any stock shares had any real value. In addition, when a stock share was purchased, the water company had to be able to deliver the water to the stockholder. They couldn't deliver water until irrigation water was available in the lakes, a term referred to as *adjudicated*[13] water.

By January 1899, the company had increased their capitalization to a total of 810 stock shares, and that number of shares has remained fixed since then. In 1886, a share of SCD&RC stock was valued at $10. Today, a share of the same stock is valued at $25,000 or more. All 810 shares are issued, so when a share is sold today, much like real estate, the "market" determines the sale price.

Even though William Womack had shares of Surface Creek Ditch and Reservoir Company water, he filed on five bodies of water in November 1898 that were not part of the SCD&RC system, and they were simply named Womack #1 through Womack #5. On his five reservoirs, he built dams from 10 to 20 feet high. Womack was assured of adequate irrigation water for his ranch, but reservoir headgates and water delivery systems require periodic repairs, and it was for that purpose that he and his ranch hands, along with his wife and two daughters, were working at one of his reservoirs in 1901, having earned a day off on a Sunday to do some fishing.

CHAPTER 6
William Alexander Disappears

William Alexander started the day like most others when he was at his resort on Grand Mesa. It was June 27, 1892, and he had planned a shopping trip to Delta to pick up some provisions for the hotel. At least, that was the agenda he described to others at the hotel when he hitched a team of horses to an express wagon (one of the old-style express wagons with low front wheels and the seat on the front of the body) and proceeded down the trail toward Cedaredge and Delta. He had a shopping list, prepared by Sam Cockreham,[14] a new partner/employee of the resort who owned the adjacent 160 acres, which also included a portion of Alexander Lake.

When Alexander reached the Hartland Ditch in north Delta, he left the wagon behind, saddled one of the team horses, and proceeded on to Delta, leading the other horse. He apparently intended to use the second mount as a packhorse for the provisions he was to purchase in Delta.

When the Hartland Ditch was built in 1890, it was 10 feet wide at the bottom, 15 feet wide at the top, and only 2½ feet deep. The headgate was (and still is) off the Gunnison River. Spring runoff would certainly have filled the river and the headgate may have been wide open, making travel by wagon across the ditch extremely dangerous, if not impossible.

The Hartland Ditch did not cross the normal wagon road between Grand Mesa and Delta, and there was no bridge over it. Normally, Alexander would have traveled most of the way over the former military road, which crossed the Gunnison just south of Austin, and then into Delta. Bridges across the Gunnison were built in 1890, both in Austin and in north Delta. The north Delta detour was probably a shortcut familiar to Alexander, and since he knew that he could not cross the ditch with his wagon, his plan was to cross on horseback, while leading the second horse of the team.

Why he left the wagon behind is, perhaps, further proof that he never intended to return. A wagon would restrict his travel to existing roads and would make it difficult if he wanted to move around off-road in relative secrecy. He had traveled to Delta many times by wagon, hauling fish for delivery to nearby towns or the train depot. And even though late-June snow runoff filled the local streams and creeks, he had certainly dealt with this issue before.

William Alexander failed to return to the hotel on Grand Mesa that same day, and the following day, it was decided to retrace his steps, thinking perhaps he had wagon problems or there was some other reason why he was unable to complete his journey. The wagon was finally found at the same place Alexander had left it, but there was no trace of him or the two horses. There did not seem to be any formal investigation of his disappearance, though there was plenty of speculation and gossip regarding it. Some said he had been murdered, while others claimed he had skipped the country for reasons of his own. No Delta County newspaper spanning that particular time frame exists in any archive, so it is unknown whether the story was a headline event or not.

Perhaps the earlier incident in 1891 was still stirring in Alexander's mind relative to getting caught with illegally farmed fish. Did it set the stage for his unannounced departure in 1892? Or maybe Alexander saw no way to pay Forrest the $2,500 required by their partnership agreement, now that the profits from selling his fish were somewhat diminished. Whatever the reason, the seed was likely planted, perhaps not consciously yet, to remove himself from the entire operation. He had only one season of operation of the new hotel at the resort—the summer of 1891—and about the time the 1892 season was to open, he disappeared.

The timing of his disappearance becomes somewhat confusing, because county agricultural records show in 1892 that William Alexander had 80 acres of irrigated pasture, grew 6

CHAPTER 6: William Alexander Disappears

acres of alfalfa, had 4 acres of orchards, produced 100 pounds of butter, and had 2 dairy cows, 17 horses, and 2 head of cattle. He could not have produced such agricultural results on Grand Mesa. Where, then, did he have a farm, and how was he able to complete the farming cycle for that year?

Under the provisions of the partnership agreement that he and Richard Forrest executed in November 1891, Alexander owned an undivided half interest in Richard Forrest's farm. Perhaps that is where he conducted his farming endeavor, though I would have thought he was rather busy at his resort, preparing for the opening in June 1892.

County records also show that he sat on a county court jury early in 1892, for which he was paid the standard $2 juror fee, as well as $13.60 for a juror certificate. Also, between July 1889 and March 1892, Alexander was paid $350 by the county for work on county roads, and it is likely that he worked on the road to his resort on Grand Mesa. William Alexander, from all appearances, appeared to be an average citizen of that time.

William Alexander's disappearance seemed to occur at a time when he was getting more involved in community responsibilities, farming, and his resort. Here one day, gone the next—forever!

For Richard Forrest, it was a difficult time. For one thing, Forrest was not used to staying at the resort—that was the role Alexander played. While both men were single, Forrest had a farm in Eckert to operate, and he did not want to be away from his farm obligations full-time during the summer months.

Richard Forrest continued to operate the Alexander Lake resort hotel, then referred to as the Forrest Hotel, for the next two years. No records have surfaced regarding his operation of the resort, so it is unclear how much time he actually spent on the mesa. One thing we can surmise is that it was a fairly low-key operation. People from both sides of the hill (north and south of the mesa) continued to take fish from the lakes in both legal and illegal ways, and little was done to discourage it.

With Alexander's disappearance, Forrest had some legal issues to resolve regarding ownership of the Grand Mesa property. The partnership agreement executed on November 6, 1891, gave each partner joint ownership of the other's holdings

MURDER AND MYSTERY ON GRAND MESA

Forrest Hotel. This photo was taken about 1894, when Richard Forrest was sole owner of the hotel and the Alexander Lakes property. There are no horses saddled for the three adults on the porch or the man standing near the horses, so there is no way to tell whether the riders are arriving or leaving.

Photo credit: Delta County Historical Society

in Eckert as well as Grand Mesa. In addition, according to the agreement, Alexander owed Forrest an additional $2,500 to equalize the deal, for which Forrest had obtained a mortgage deed from Alexander. None of the money owed by Alexander was ever paid.

On August 7, 1894, Forrest filed notice that he was suing Alexander to obtain a foreclosure of the mortgage owed Forrest, a legal process whereby a judgment in Forrest's favor would place the undivided half interest in the two properties in a Sheriff's Sale. On February 21, 1895, Forrest was awarded a judgment for $3,025, which included the original $2,500 plus interest that had accrued. When the case came up for sale on March 28, 1895, by Delta County Sheriff Clarence Mower, Forrest's bid of $3,000 was accepted and was simply credited against the judgment already received for $3,025. Case closed! Richard Forrest now had complete legal ownership of the Alexander Lakes property *and* his original farm in Eckert.

CHAPTER 6: William Alexander Disappears

It would be 11 years before William Alexander's name would once again appear in the Delta County newspapers. An investigation into the disappearance of William Alexander by this author produced some rather interesting information that is presented in later chapters. The reader is invited to draw their own conclusion as to whether William Alexander was ever "found."

CHAPTER 7
Fishing Law of 1893

One of the unsolved mysteries of this story is why William Alexander had a need for irrigation water back in October 1886 when he was an original stockholder and director in the Surface Creek Ditch and Reservoir Company. He had yet to claim, by preemption, any land on Grand Mesa, and would not have needed any irrigation water there, anyway. We can only assume that his need was justified, and that he lived somewhere within the jurisdiction of the SCD&RC.

As a stockholder in the SCD&RC, he had fishing rights as well as water rights in all lakes claimed by the company. By 1890, Richard Forrest was also a stockholder in the SCD&RC, and both he and Alexander were already working on improvements to Alexander's Fish Lake Resort on the mesa, now a partnership and part of the source of water owned by the ditch company. Richard Forrest did have a 160-acre claim in the Eckert area and his stock shares in the SCD&RC made sense. Alexander's shares remain a puzzle.

With the resort in full operation by the summer of 1891, Alexander and Forrest saw the value in obtaining exclusive fish culture rights within the lakes under which the SCD&RC had control of all water rights. So in March 1892, Alexander and Forrest executed a 99-year lease with the SCD&RC, whereby they surrendered their irrigation rights of the lakes in return for acquiring exclusive fish culture rights in all waters controlled by the SCD&RC, as well as retaining their fishing privileges in those waters.

A new fishing law enacted on April 8, 1893, reinforced Forrest's[15] control over the fish culture rights in the 13

CHAPTER 7: Fishing Law of 1893

reservoirs and lakes from which he and Alexander had previously leased water rights from the Surface Creek Ditch and Reservoir Company, and, oddly enough, gave them complete control of the fishing rights, as well. Did that mean that Forrest could now exclude the other stockholders from fishing in all SCD&RC reservoirs and lakes? Technically, it did!

The new law read as follows: First, it was unlawful for any person, persons, or corporation to catch or take in any way any trout or other fish by any means whatsoever from any private pond or private lake, except by the consent of the owner or proprietor of such pond or lake. Alexander and Forrest were considered to have ownership and proprietorship of three lakes, since their property included the partial shoreline of Alexander Lake and all of the shoreline of Twin Lakes; and, by virtue of the 99-year lease they held with the SCD&RC, they also had fishing and fish culture rights in all 13 lakes under SCD&RC control.

Second, in case the right to take water for irrigating purposes from any private pond or lake was in one person or corporation (that right stayed with the SCD&RC), and the right to propagate or keep fish in any such pond, lake, or stream was in another person or corporation (that right was now with Forrest), the right to fish would be obtained from the person or corporation having the right to keep and propagate fish in such pond or lake. This provision simply meant that Forrest had the right to the fish and fish culture in all 13 lakes that had been filed on by the SCD&RC for stored water for irrigation, and that anyone wishing to fish in those lakes had to have his permission. This was the provision that was the basis for most of the problems later under William Radcliffe's ownership.

Third, the person, persons or corporations owning or controlling the water stored or impounded in such pond or lake would be decreed and held to be the owner and proprietor of the fish in such pond or lake (that would be the SCD&RC), although such person, persons, or corporation may not have legal title to the ground covered by the water of such pond or lake. This provision meant that the SCD&RC owned the fish in all 13 lakes, even though they did not hold legal title to the land under the lakes—though in this matter, they had leased the fish culture rights to Alexander and Forrest for 99 years. The only interest of the SCD&RC was to the stored water in the lakes, to be used for irrigation purposes in the Surface Creek Valley.

Finally, there was a provision that any person found fishing by hook and line, seine, or otherwise in any such private pond or lake, without the consent of the owner or proprietor of the pond or lake, would be deemed guilty of a misdemeanor, and on conviction thereof would be fined not less than $10 and not more than $20 for the first offense, and not less than $25 and not more than $50 for each subsequent offense. Half of such a fine would go to the owner or proprietor of the pond or lake, and the other half would go to the benefit of the school fund of the county where the fishing was done.

There is no evidence that Forrest ever really enforced this new law with regard to anglers requesting permission from him to fish in any of the 13 lakes. First of all, he had no resources to enforce the law, and more important, no one would have followed such a ruling. For over 12 years, the pioneer citizens had fished the Grand Mesa lakes at their whim, using both legal and illegal methods, and they considered the lakes and the fish in them to be public property. At the same time, Forrest realized that the lakes and reservoirs would eventually be fished out, so their focus was more on the fish hatchery operation to keep the resort a viable and profitable business.

The 1893 law may have been the result of the creation of the Battlement Mesa Forest Reserve in 1892 and the subsequent control of the forest reserve by the government. All of the Grand Mesa land was federally owned at the outset, by virtue of the fact that it had been part of the Consolidated Ute (Indian) Reservation, and even though the reservation was dissolved, the land remained under federal ownership and control. The government sold land parcels under such programs as the Preemption Act, the Desert Land Act, and the Homestead Act.

When William Alexander disappeared in June 1892, the fish culture provision of the law was actively continued by Richard Forrest, but he exercised no control over any fishing. His fish hatchery operation could not keep up with the amount of fish taken out of the lakes, and fishing simply got worse. Since his

CHAPTER 7: Fishing Law of 1893

hotel was at Alexander Lake, much of the fry ended up being placed there. However, a "fry" did not become a legal catchable fish for about three years, so his early hatchery endeavors had yet to change the fishing situation.

From the perspective of the average angler, not much had changed.

CHAPTER 8

Sam Cockreham Sells His Claim

Pioneer Samuel L. Cockreham first shows up in Delta County in the early 1890s. He had settled in the Hotchkiss area and, while living there, had met and married Sarah Viola Allen on July 7, 1891. Within a year of his marriage, Samuel Cockreham filed by preemption on 160 acres of land on Grand Mesa. adjoining the parcel owned by William Alexander, and on October 29, 1892, received his Receiver's Receipt, meaning that he had met the legal requirements for full ownership of his land by paying $206.44 for his 165.15 acres. Cockreham's claim included a portion of Alexander Lake, most of Barren Lake, and the west end of Eggleston Lake.

Cockreham could not have received his Receiver's Receipt without first building a cabin on his claim. He and William Alexander were "neighbors" at a time when few others even visited Grand Mesa. Perhaps they had both wintered there in 1889 or 1890.

While Cockreham was not in the fish culture business, we do know that he became a partner—or more properly, an employee with the Alexander resort operation, though the relationship did not involve any joint ownership of the real estate. That was the Alexander-Forrest partnership only. Cockreham apparently worked at the Alexander Hotel in some capacity, since he was the person who prepared the shopping list for Alexander on the day that Alexander disappeared.

Cockreham's property on Grand Mesa had been occupied and operated by E.C. Teachout as a summer resort, though it lacked a hotel like the adjoining Alexander property. Cockreham did not live full-time on his Grand Mesa property, as he also had a place in the Hotchkiss area.

CHAPTER 8: Sam Cockreham Sells His Claim

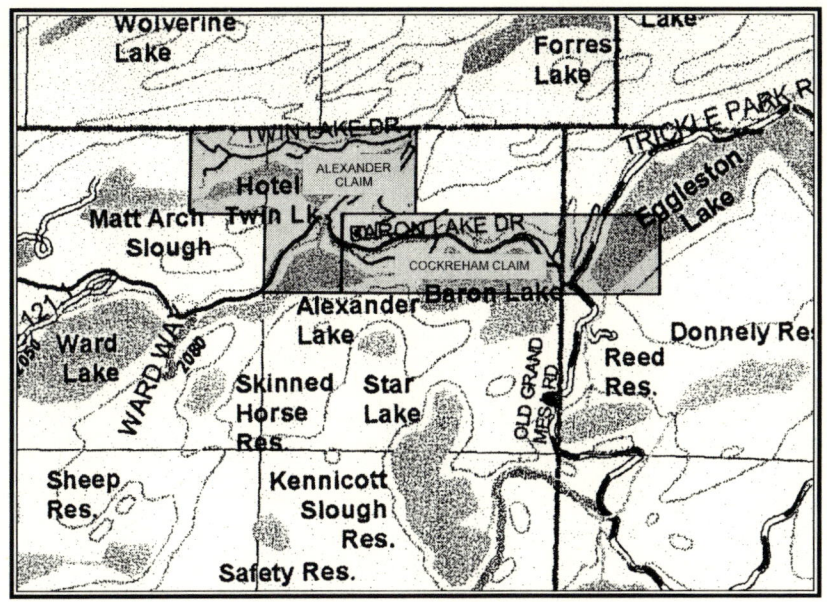

Map showing the property preempted by both William Alexander and Sam Cockreham, a total of 325 acres. This acreage today is completely surrounded by national forest land, and is still the only property within this forest that is privately owned, grandfathered because it predated the formation of the Battlement Mesa Forest Preserve in 1892.

Credit: Author

When the state fish and game laws were revised in 1893, Sam Cockreham came up with the idea to sell his claim to a group of men who formed a stock company and who thought they had an opportunity to take advantage of the new fishing law by becoming joint proprietors of the fishing in "their" lakes for their own recreation. Sam Cockreham was also given stock in the company. Allegedly, this deal was put through largely on account of the attempts made by Richard Forrest to monopolize all the fishing ground in the vicinity. Forrest owned the land adjoining this and claimed to have stocked the lakes with fish.

By Quit Claim Deed, Cockreham sold his land for a consideration of $600 on December 4, 1893, to 15 men, all citizens of Delta County. They were: G. Wright, C.E. Wetzel, I.M. Conklin, Ben S. Gheen, G.C. Gule, H.H. Wolbert, W. Ray Simpson, H.C. Bear, O.J. Standish, J.A. Curtis, R.S. Kellog, H. Fogg, C.J. Johnson, I.M. McMurray, and George H. Duke.

MURDER AND MYSTERY ON GRAND MESA

All of these men were business leaders in Delta County, and all were sportsmen who loved to get away to Grand Mesa for fishing and hunting recreation. As a partnership, they called themselves the "Grand Mesa Resort Company." Some of the partners constructed cabins, a few of which survive to this day.

A few years later, when William Radcliffe succeeded to the Alexander Lakes property and the fishing rights that went with it, the shareholders of the Grand Mesa Resort Company resisted his pretentions to an exclusive fishing right in their lakes, but to no avail: Radcliffe had the law on his side. But the 15 men maintained their company structure, in spite of Radcliffe, which would prove to be of value years later.

If any of the 15 men who formed the Grand Mesa Resort Company were worried about future problems with Richard Forrest, their concerns were probably set at ease when the following snippet appeared in *The Delta Independent* in May 1894:

> *The anticipated quarrel between Dick Forrest and the boys who wish to fish on the old Cockreham ranch on Grand Mesa will no doubt be suppressed. Mr. Forrest seems to be willing that they should enjoy themselves on the hill all they wish, and the boys are not going to be obstinate in any of their demands. The indications are that there will be plenty of sport and not a cross word on the mesa this summer.*

True to his word, Forrest left the Grand Mesa Resort Company alone, and both resorts seemed to operate without conflict for the next two years. Then an Englishman named William Radcliffe entered the scene.

CHAPTER 9

Richard Forrest— New Responsibilities

It is believed that Richard Forrest spent some time in the Gunnison, Colorado, area following his Denver shipping ventures, and he was certainly aware that the Western Slope of Colorado was rid of the Ute Indians and that the area offered fine farmland for settlement. However, it would be three to four years before he would make the move to Delta County.

About the same time Forrest was moving to Delta County, Mary Magdeline Ungerman was traveling from Spring City, Utah, to Gunnison to care for two of her brothers who were miners there by keeping house for them—basically cooking meals for them. The Denver & Rio Grande Railroad had reached Gunnison in 1877, four years before the Utes were escorted to the Uintah Reservation in Utah. The early narrow gauge railroad extended to Montrose, Delta, and Grand Junction in 1882, so it is likely that Mary Ungerman traveled to Gunnison by way of Salt Lake City, Grand Junction, Delta, Montrose, and on to Gunnison. She traveled with her parents, Henning and Christina Olsen-Ungerman,[16] as Mary was only 19 years old in 1885.

Family records reveal that Mary and her two brothers traveled one day to Delta, Colorado, and booked accommodations in the Delta House hotel. The Delta House was built in 1890 and, from the start, was Delta's finest hotel, catering to businessmen and travelers alike. Apparently it was a family reunion of sorts, as their mother and father met them there, as well. That same evening, Richard Forrest was in the hotel, probably enjoying an excellent meal for which the Delta House[17] was well known.

Mary apparently spotted Forrest and turned to one of her brothers and asked, "Do you know that man?", to which he replied that he did not. Mary then said, "Well, get acquainted with him and introduce him to me, for that is the man I am going to marry."

From this meeting, a relationship developed, and on April 4, 1895, Richard Forrest and Mary M. Ungerman were married in Eckert, Colorado. Perhaps it was this pending marriage that caused Forrest to file the lawsuit in Delta's court system against his former partner, William Alexander, to claim Alexander's portion of the land and property holdings. Alexander had been gone three years now, and it was time to resolve the property holdings issue created by the partnership agreement executed in 1891, as well as the joint ownership executed through legal Warranty Deeds. In addition, Forrest, no doubt, wanted this all to be settled before his marriage.

Forrest's marriage in April 1895 likely put a damper on his willingness to spend much time on the mesa running the resort. It also meant that without his hands-on operation, he would have little control over the financial end of the business. Perhaps this was the moment when he decided to sell the resort, and he may have even advertised his intention. Little did he know there was a man waiting in the area for just this opportunity.

Marriage Certificate of Richard and Mary (Ungerman) Forrest. They were married on April 4, 1895.

Credit: Delta County Clerk and Recorder Office

CHAPTER 10

William Radcliffe Appears

The Delta Independent announced it first, on October 30, 1895: "Dick Forrest has sold his lake property to Mr. William Radcliffe." What started off as a simple announcement soon developed into the talk of the county. No one would really know anything about William Radcliffe until late June of 1896, since he did not spend any time around the county until then.

Alexander Lake and a distant view of the resort built by Alexander and Forrest. This photo, originally a post card, was taken about 1895. The fish hatchery is the log structure near the lake shore.
Photo credit: Delta County Historical Society

MURDER AND MYSTERY ON GRAND MESA

Actually, in October 1895, Richard Forrest had agreed to the sale, but it did not officially take place until May 14, 1896. Radcliffe paid $7,000 cash for the 162 acres on Grand Mesa. The Warranty Deed transferring the property specifically excluded the 99-year lease with the Surface Creek Ditch and Reservoir Company and the fish and fish culture benefits included with it. That transaction, also conducted May 14, was by Quit Claim Deed for which another $7,000 in consideration was paid by Radcliffe. The Quit Claim Deed transferred the 99-year lease, as well as the fishing rights and fish culture rights previously owned by Forrest, for 17 reservoirs then under the control of the SCD&RC.

William Radcliffe, the man who purchased the resort property from Richard Forrest, had already established a presence in the area, having purchased a 160-acre parcel by Quit Claim Deed from Alfred Botsford on June 24, 1895. Botsford was a cattleman with over 500 acres of land in the Harts Basin area, just east of Eckert, and a neighbor of Richard Forrest at the time. This acreage, for which Radcliffe paid $5,000, was located northwest of Eckert in an area with no water available via streams, except that he had rights on the nearby Cedar Park Ditch.

In July 1898, Radcliffe paid another $1,000 to the Delta County Bank from which he obtained a Warranty Deed for the same land, though it is not clear why he did not have clear title to the land by virtue of the earlier Quit Claim Deed. Today, this parcel would be in the middle of Colby Canyon. Perhaps Radcliffe planned to use this acreage as a hunting and game preserve, as that was one of his passions. He certainly would have either visited the Alexander-Forrest resort on Grand Mesa, or perhaps heard about it at the Denver Club that he frequented whenever in the Denver area. His attention was heightened upon learning of the superior fishing and game opportunities on Grand Mesa. So when he heard of the opportunity to purchase the Grand Mesa operation, he probably started the proverbial wheels-in-motion and began to make plans almost immediately.

No record has been found that Radcliffe ever used his Colby Canyon land for any purpose. After his purchase of the resort on the mesa, it undoubtedly kept him busy during the season, since

CHAPTER 10: William Radcliffe Appears

it provided fishing and hunting, both passions of his. He did not winter in the Delta County area, either, and finally sold the Colby Canyon property in September 1900 for $4,500.

Who was William Radcliffe? William M. Radcliffe was born August 12, 1856, on the island of Jamaica in the British West Indies, and thus was a British subject. He was the last of seven children born to his mother, Jane (Wilson) Radcliffe. His mother and two of his siblings, eight-year-old twins, died in 1856, probably the result of an accident. Both his father, John Radcliffe, and his mother were born in Ireland. John Radcliffe died in 1892 at the age of 77.

At age 40, William Radcliffe was often described as an English aristocrat. He was a graduate from London's Oxford

William Radcliffe sketch prepared by a reporter for the Rocky Mountain News, *that was published in 1901 after the burning of his hotel on Grand Mesa. No other photos of Radcliffe, while he was in Colorado, are known to exist.*
Photo credit: Denver Public Library, Western History Department

University, 5 feet 10 inches tall, distinguished looking and athletic, with white hair, white mustache and eyebrows, and gray-blue eyes. He was accustomed to wealth and had paid cash for all of his land holdings. His travels took him all over the globe, and he was an accomplished linguist and interesting conversationalist. He was a true sportsman, was an ardent hunter and fisherman and knowledgeable about both, and he was reported to be an excellent horseman. He always wore beautifully tailored clothes, which were fashioned of heavy Scotch and English fabrics.

Although he owned real estate in England and Ireland, his summers would be spent in Colorado, and the rest of the year in Paris or in his luxurious apartment in London. When in Denver, he always put up at the Denver Club, even though he was not a member. The Denver Club was host to wealthy and important influential men in the area, and Radcliffe felt "at home" in their midst.

From the start, Radcliffe leased the Alexander Lakes hotel to a man who had experience in operating one, as he did not

Grand Mesa Hotel. This view of the hotel was probably captured about the time William Radcliffe bought the resort—in 1896. It is interesting to note the number of smaller children in this photo, suggesting that their trip to the hotel was likely in a buggy and not on horseback. In this photo, the hotel is identified as the Grand Mesa Hotel.

Photo credit: Delta County Historical Society

CHAPTER 10: William Radcliffe Appears

see himself as a hotel manager. His passion was fishing and hunting in this setting. He placed the hotel under the supervision of Newton Smith, who had been running the Commercial Hotel in Delta for the past year and a half. Radcliffe advertised that patrons of his hotel would find many improvements this season, and Smith planned to open the hotel for the reception of guests about the fifteenth of June. For those staying at the hotel, boating and fishing were to be free.

Radcliffe also placed A.T. Francis in charge of the hatchery. He was already making plans to increase the hatchery capability to 1,250,000 fish and had made arrangements with the U.S. Fish and Game Commission for a consignment of eastern and rainbow trout. It would not be long, however, before Radcliffe would begin to experience some of the same problems as those of Alexander and Forrest. He would soon learn that pioneer westerners simply did not play by the same rules as British aristocrats.

William Radcliffe arrived from England about the first of June 1896, the same day the fishing season was open. One of the first things he did was to announce that those interested in the lakes would be allowed free fishing privileges on application to the manager at the hotel, and those found fishing without permits would be "looked after" by the deputy game warden, claiming this action was necessary to protect the fish until the lakes were well-stocked.

Radcliffe was especially conspicuous when at his ranch on the mesa. There he dressed like an English huntsman: scarlet coat, light whipcord trousers, polished boots, and velvet hat, and he carried an elaborate hunting bag. In addition, his taste for scotch and soda and monogrammed cigarettes from Picadilly did not exactly endear him to his neighbors on Grand Mesa.

He was not fully satisfied with the agreement that permitted the SCD&RC stockholders to fish unrestricted, for practically every man on the mesa claimed this right. His idea, from the beginning, was to make a vast private park of the area, his own baronial estate. This, the Delta and Mesa County people bitterly resented, and Radcliffe, experiencing the same trouble with poachers as had his predecessors, hired watchmen, or guards, to patrol the lakes and arrest anyone found fishing without a permit. This was an additional thorn in the flesh of the Surface

Creek Ditch and Reservoir stockholders and of the people of Delta County generally, who earlier camped at the Grand Mesa lakes, fishing whenever they pleased. To many of them, it was not a matter of sport, but of food, and there were no other lakes where fish abounded in the vicinity. They claimed that when the trout went to spawn up the streams that united and formed Tongue Creek, a tributary of the Gunnison River, Radcliffe sent men to seine the fish, claiming they were his. He, in turn, charged that they not only seined but dynamited and used grab hooks, violating the law.

Arrests for trespassing on the grounds and waters were made, but there were no convictions, owing, said Radcliffe, to the strong feeling against the closing of the lakes. Feelings grew more and more tense. The case against Otto C. Petersen of Cedaredge and his son, which attracted general attention, resulted in dismissal, the jury failing to convict. William A. Womack, one of the jurors and an original stockholder, especially resented what he considered the curtailment of his privileges.

A well-to-do cattleman in his early fifties, Womack had come from Texas in 1889 and lived with his wife and eight children near Eckert, and his cattle range was in the neighborhood of the lakes. Radcliffe knew Womack's name well, apparently the result of encounters between Womack and some of Radcliffe's employees. One such encounter was soon to have a fatal ending.

CHAPTER 11

William A. Womack— Cattleman

In Texas, William A. Womack was a cotton farmer. With help from his wife, Eliza, and eight children, they were able to save a little money, but corn and cotton prices were so low that they decided to head west. They were prepared to travel all the way to the northwest country. When the Womack family left Texas, they traveled with the Cole family, a total of 24 people in all. The travelers also had 310 cattle and some cows, horses, and oxen.

The group departed Texas on April 1, 1889. Along the way, they encountered Chocktaw, Chickasha, Kiowa, and Comanche Indians as they traveled through their respective territories, but it was the Comanches that gave them some anxious moments, taking some of their food and cattle, without interference on the part of the Womack-Cole party. If they had objected or even raised weapons in the process, they would likely not have survived, being greatly outnumbered.

When they reached Trinidad, Colorado, they were told by an unscrupulous citizen that Colorado had no grass and that the whole place was adobe hills, so they sold all but 24 of their cattle out of fear that there would be insufficient food for them, taking a huge financial loss in the process. As they continued their journey, they realized their mistake in selling most of the cattle. Colorado did, indeed, have good grass, and plenty of it! They continued on to Del Norte, where the Cole family decided to settle, and the Womacks continued on to Delta. Oddly enough, Delta did not appeal to them at the time, so they continued on to Grand Mesa, where they camped for the remainder of the summer.

MURDER AND MYSTERY ON GRAND MESA

The Womack family probably met William Alexander that fall and were introduced to the activities of the Surface Creek Ditch and Reservoir Company, as well. They soon located on the Bar I ranch in Cedaredge and probably lived and worked there for the next year, until William Womack had time to find some good land that met his ranching needs. In March 1890, Womack purchased a building in Delta across from the Delta House and operated a dry goods business over the summer. He apparently did not care for the rigors of running a retail business and sold it in September.

It is possible that William Womack and his family were simply adjusting to the area and weren't sure that Delta County was to remain their new home. Apparently they made a decision to stay over the winter of 1890-91, and in May 1891, he purchased a 160-acre parcel about two miles northwest of Eckert.

Womack was not one to pass up income opportunities, and in October 1893, he bid and won a contract to furnish coal for the county offices in Delta—14 tons of coal, more or less, at $3.75 a ton from the Winton Mine. It was hardly a real money maker, but with eight children to feed, it probably provided a few groceries to fill some hungry stomachs.

Then in August 1894, Womack preempted another 160 acres adjoining the first parcel, followed by the purchase of a third 160-acre piece in January 1898 a half mile distant from the previous 320 acres. Womack now had 480 acres of land and was just starting to grow his cattle herd.

Also in 1898, Womack filed on five small bodies of water on the south face of Grand Mesa and made plans to create reservoirs for the storage of irrigation water needed for his ranch. His reservoirs, identified as Womack #1 through Womack #5, are today just #1 and #2. The original five reservoirs became merged into just two reservoirs when dams 10 to 20 feet high were built on the two biggest, and he was able to capture sufficient water to meet not only his needs, but others, as well.

A year earlier, county agricultural records revealed that, even by 1897, Womack had 100 acres irrigated and 180 acres of pasture, plus acreage of wheat, oats, and alfalfa, as well as a 14-acre orchard. Like many other ranchers, Womack also had summer cattle range on Grand Mesa, and his was in the

CHAPTER 11: William A. Womack—Cattleman

vicinity of the Grand Mesa lakes group. By 1901, his cattle herd had grown to over 400 head, and as any cattle rancher knows, such a herd requires lots of feed and plenty of water to grow the feed. Womack apparently had both, though it was work on one of his reservoirs that brought him to the mesa with his wife, two daughters, and a few of his cow hands on a warm July day in 1901. It was a day that made history, though William A. Womack would never see another sunrise.

CHAPTER 12

Radcliffe Makes New Rules

When William Radcliffe assumed ownership of the Alexander Lakes property from Richard Forrest, he found lakes that were virtually fished out. At his best, Forrest's hatchery at Alexander Lake had only seven troughs for producing fry from trout eggs, resulting in only about 200,000 fry a season. This was barely enough to keep the three lakes controlled by Forrest with enough mature trout for drawing fishermen to his resort for the recreation of hook-and-line fishing.

Even before Alexander's disappearance in 1892, he and Forrest had no way to police their lakes for illegal fishing. When Radcliffe took over, he found dynamite fuses, gunnysacks, nets, and other illegal "tools" that, while not commonly used under Forrest's ownership, were nevertheless used enough that the fish population did not increase.

Fish were even depleted from some of the streams, and no effort was made to distinguish between the females with eggs or any others. Fish were fish, and there were those people who simply temporarily dammed or diverted streams such that, when the water ran out along the normal course, the fish were revealed and sometimes clubbed or gathered in gunnysacks. On a good day, and under the right conditions, someone could illegally snare enough fish to feed their family for a year, taking hundreds of pounds of fish at a time. Fish were preserved by the process of smoking, much like other meats then and even today.

Alexander and Forrest owned the fish in their three lakes. According to the fish and game laws of the time, they could legally sell fish obtained from their lakes. However, in order to

CHAPTER 12: Radcliffe Makes New Rules

secure enough fish at a given time to take to market, it was easier to seine the fish from the streams leaving their lake—but the streams were considered public waters, from which it was illegal to "catch" and sell fish.

For this reason, when Alexander was caught selling illegally caught fish in Leadville, he was arrested and charged with a violation of the state fishing laws, for which he had to pay a hefty fine—for those times. When Alexander disappeared a year later, his resort, then operated by Forrest, no longer sold fish by the pound, but dealt only with fish culture—the hatchery—and the resort hotel.

Under Radcliffe's supervision, the fish hatchery operation was gearing up for a substantial increase in fish culture, and he was in the early stages of building up the fish population in his lakes. From the start, Radcliffe began increasing the capability of his fish hatchery operation. In his first year, 1896, he added 28 additional troughs, which brought his egg capacity up to about 4,000,000, but that year he only farmed about 1,000,000 eggs. Radcliffe was aware that under the Alexander-Forrest ownership of the lakes, the fish population was greatly reduced. The hatchery under their ownership just could not keep up with the depletion of mature fish by dynamiting, seining, and other illegal means.

Being the sportsman that he was, Radcliffe was not allowing any of that type of fishing. For that reason, he began to hire game wardens. Even at this early stage of his business, he required people to have a permit to fish in his lakes, which his office freely issued on request. Radcliffe could also refuse to issue a permit, though there is no historical evidence that he ever did this. There was no cost for a permit and, like any good politician, he delivered permits to county officials and others who he felt he might need on his side, even if they did not fish. Current fishing laws made no mention of permits being required. That was Radcliffe's rule, and one that was strongly resented by everyone. There were reports that Radcliffe's permits specified which lakes the holder of the permit was allowed to fish in. Many felt he specified lakes "as devoid of fish as the adobe deserts."

MURDER AND MYSTERY ON GRAND MESA

His second year of production in 1897 was a failure because he was unable to secure spawn, hatching only 225 trout. However, in 1898 he turned out 900,000 trout, and in 1899, over one million.

Special game wardens were appointed by the state, though they acted under the orders of, and were paid by, the proprietor of the preserve. As part of their duties, Radcliffe required his wardens to ride (by horseback) the lake shores to ascertain whether all persons fishing or planning to fish were in possession of the proper permit. A person in violation of the permit rule would be asked to desist or become a prisoner, taken to jail, and prosecuted in the courts.

When Frank Mahany was hired by the state to work for Radcliffe as a Deputy Game Warden, he was supposedly hired because a number of Delta citizens had, by petition, specifically asked for him. Perhaps it was odd that some of the people who signed the petition were those who might have violated the permit rules. Or maybe there was no petition at all. Newspapers of the time (like today) often had statements printed that had no basis in truth.

In the July 1, 1897 issue of *The Delta Laborer,* the following was printed:

> *NOTICE TO THE PUBLIC: Fishing at Alexander Lakes, Season of 1897.*
>
> *In consequence of wrong impressions prevailing as regards fishing privilege therein, the proprietors of the fishing rights in the reservoirs of Grand Mesa wish it to be understood that to residents of Delta county who wish to fish with hook and line for their own use, cards of permission will be granted to enjoy that privilege upon application to the proprietors or their agents at the hotel or hatcheries.*
>
> *In order to prevent the destruction of fish it has become necessary to stop unlawful fishing, and the purchasers of the fishing privileges formerly enjoyed by Forrest and Alexander, particularly request all good people to aid them, both by refraining from fishing on their premises without permission, and by reporting to the State Game and Fish Wardens appointed for the neighborhood, any violation of the law.*

CHAPTER 12: Radcliffe Makes New Rules

In a letter dated July 2, 1897, which William Radcliffe sent to the editor of *The Delta Laborer* newspaper for publication on July 8, he stated:

> *Dear Sir: While in Delta yesterday I was told by one of the citizens of that place that $500.00, of which he would give $10.00, could be raised in two hours to get a decision as to fishing rights in Alexander Lakes. I am writing you that in view of this, I will give every facility in my power toward securing such an action and decision from the United States Court. I am writing the game warden to the same effect, and I trust you will acknowledge that on my part I have not confined myself to carping talk but have tried to do all I can to establish the rights in this case. I appeal to you to use your influence for a just hearing and a publication of this letter in your next issue of the Laborer. Please show this to anyone and everybody you like.*
>
> *Yours truly,*
> *Wm. Radcliffe*

Radcliffe seldom used the newspapers to air his problems, but July 1897 seemed to be a month when he chose to communicate in that fashion. He also placed the following ad in *The Delta Laborer* of July 23, 1897:

> Alexander Lakes:
> The Hotel is now open for the season with an experienced cook at the head of the culinary department.
>
> Good Table:
> Six boats; fishing free to all guests of the hotel. Two cottages to let furnished. Single cottages $3.50 per week. Double cottage, $7.00 per week.
> Apply to
>   Wm Radcliffe, Alexander Lakes

In the September 24, 1897 issue of *The Delta Independent*, a letter from Fish Commissioner J.S. Swan was printed that didn't necessarily settle the issue legally, but did absolve Radcliffe's actions. It read, in part:

MURDER AND MYSTERY ON GRAND MESA

Commissioner, Forestry, Game and Fish, Colorado
Denver, August 25, 1897

In the matter of ownership of the Alexander Lakes, on Grand Mesa, Delta County, and the fish therein, which matter was brought to my attention by you in a letter to this department in June last, I have decided not to disturb the present title, presumptively vested in W. Radcliffe, as the lessee of the Surface Creek Ditch and Reservoir Co.

In arriving at this decision, I have endeavored to be governed by law, at the same time being mindful of the equities involved and the public interest.

Sometime in July last, ..., I requested Mr. E.F. Campbell, State Supt. Of Hatcheries, to visit Delta and also the lakes and from every source of information collect all data that might be of assistance in ascertaining the rightful ownership of said lakes.

In 1895 Alexander & Forrest, ..., sold and transferred to W. Radcliffe, Esq., all their interest in said lease.

On June 7, 1895, the former commissioner of this department ... confirmed the title now claimed by Mr. Radcliffe.

Mr. Radcliffe allows the public to fish with hook and line, but asks the persons desiring such privilege to get a permit from him. Notices are posted throughout the grounds warning persons that it is private property and no fishing allowed without such permit.

I find that since his purchase from Alexander & Forrest in 1895, Mr. Radcliffe has increased his hatcheries from 7 to 31 hatching troughs and at the time of my visit had in the hatchery over 200,000 fry which he was placing in the lakes. He had in his employ and pay a number of special game wardens for the protection of fish in the lakes.

The letter went on to say that he (Swan) had submitted the question of legality to the state attorney general, and his reply stated:

CHAPTER 12: Radcliffe Makes New Rules

Our conclusion is, therefore, that the Surface Creek Ditch and Reservoir Co., holding possessory right to the land, or their lessee, Mr. Wm. Radcliffe, is entitled to all fish rights in said lakes to the exclusion of the public.

Swan wrapped up his letter by stating:

As the public of Delta County has heretofore been granted the privilege of fishing in said lakes by permit from Mr. Radcliffe upon request for same, I would suggest that such arrangement be continued until such time as every doubt of title as between Mr. Radcliffe and the state be laid by a possible future determination of the matter by the Courts.

It was not what the citizens of Delta County wanted to read that day, and it did nothing to diminish the feelings that prevailed against Radcliffe. Moreover, it did not stop some of the anglers from ignoring this ruling and fishing anyway, hoping to avoid Radcliffe's game wardens in the process. Thirteen lakes and only six game wardens: They couldn't be everywhere at once. Though there was a lot of resistance to the permit rule, the majority of the citizens complied with it.

But the situation also created another problem. Radcliffe did not control all the lakes, and those with fish were heavily fished, including the use of dynamite and nets. After a while, Radcliffe's lakes were the best fishing on the mesa, since he restocked them periodically with fry from his hatchery. The state was responsible for restocking the other lakes, and the Grand Mesa lakes were only a portion of their responsibility.

For his first three seasons of operation, Radcliffe focused his energy on improving his fish hatchery operation and selling fish from his lakes to distant markets. His relationship with the Fish and Game Commission was good, and his hatchery had contracts with the state hatchery in Leadville.

But there were changes in the wind, and with the assistance of Radcliffe's Denver attorney, David C. Beaman—a known fish and game expert—new fishing laws were being crafted that, when enacted by the Colorado legislature, were to set in motion even more conflict between Radcliffe and the men and women who fished the Grand Mesa lakes under his control.

CHAPTER 13

Fishing Laws Change Again in 1899

On April 27, 1899, a new fishing law was enacted called the "Beaman Law." It may as well have been called the Radcliffe-Beaman law, because Radcliffe and Beaman, a good friend of Radcliffe, collaborated on the law's content. David C. Beaman was a prominent attorney, a sportsman of Denver, and a legal advisor to the Colorado Fuel & Iron Company. He was also a shrewd politician of sorts and managed to carry the law to a colleague in the Colorado legislature. Though the law creating and authorizing "private preserves" passed the legislature and was enacted by the governor, it was one that the fishing public considered discriminating and inflammatory, affecting individual rights.

At that time it seemed innocent enough, but it contained a controversial provision in the form of a clause (Division C, Section Four) that read: "The provisions of this division in relation to private parks and lakes, the licensing thereof for the keeping and propagation of game or fish therein, and permitting the sale thereof, shall apply to every park or lake in whole or in part thereof on land held by private ownership, and to every lake the water of which, or the right to the use of such water, in whole or in part, has been or may hereafter be acquired under the laws of the state or the United States, for irrigation purposes, and the owner of such land or water rights shall be deemed the proprietor of such park or lake, and the game or fish therein and such lakes shall be designated as Class A."

In simpler language, the 1899 law allowed for the private lease of a lake or lakes for the purpose of fish propagation, allowed the lessee to keep such lake or lakes stocked at the state's

CHAPTER 13: Fishing Laws Change Again in 1899

expense—allowing the lessee a little better fishing than others—and lastly, it allowed the lessee to take fish and sell them in the open markets year round, without regard to open or closed season for fishing. The lessee had only to obtain a "private fishing park license" from the state and pay a nominal fee for it. The lessee was also obligated to protect the fish and to give back to the state 10 percent of the eggs obtained for the state hatchery.

On June 4, 1899, Radcliffe, taking advantage of the leasing section of this law, secured from Game Commissioner Johnson a "Class A" license for a period of 10 years, which gave him complete control and ownership of the fish in the lakes, as a part of each of the lakes over which he claimed jurisdiction was on his land covered by his lease. The land really did border on these lakes, but many of the lakes also touched land other than that under lease to Radcliffe.

Radcliffe was the second person in the state of Colorado to apply for a license under the new law, and for a fee of $145, he was able to lease 13 prime lakes on Grand Mesa, which also included the rivers and streams connecting the lakes. He owned part of the real estate on only three of them. If another person owned the real estate surrounding one of the lakes, that person had no rights to the fish in the lake, even though it was actually on his property.

Radcliffe's Class A license read as follows:

STATE OF COLORADO
DEPARTMENT OF GAME AND FISH
Denver, May 4, 1899

This certifies that William Radcliffe, proprietor of 13 private lakes called Alexander, etc., as per application, and situated on secs. 31 and 32, T11S, R94W; sec 36, T11S, R95W; secs. 5 and 6, T12S, R94W; and secs. 1,2,3,9,10 and 11, T12S, R95W, in Delta County, Colo., is hereby authorized to keep and propagate therein and dispose of as provided by law, the following fish, viz:

Mountain trout and other fish, together with such additions thereto (with the natural increase of all) as may hereafter be lawfully acquired.

MURDER AND MYSTERY ON GRAND MESA

This authorizes possession, use, and sale, but not transportation, and expires ten years after date.

T.H. JOHNSON, Commissioner

Put in simpler terms, Radcliffe's preserve license covered 11 square miles, or 7,040 acres. Not bad for a man that had purchased only 162 acres a few years earlier and, for a fee of $145, expanded that coverage as already noted.

The string of lakes owned by Radcliffe included Alexander, Barren, Eggleston, Upper Eggleston, Hotel, Upper Hotel, Island, Deep Slough, Sheep Slough, Carp, Beaver, and Beaver Dam. It was estimated by Colorado Game Commissioner Johnson that there were about 800,000 mountain trout in the lakes.

For most, the new law made no sense. Here was a man named William Radcliffe who, by virtue of having paid the state of Colorado $145 to lease thirteen lakes, legally owned the lakes and the fish in the lakes, but did not necessarily own the real

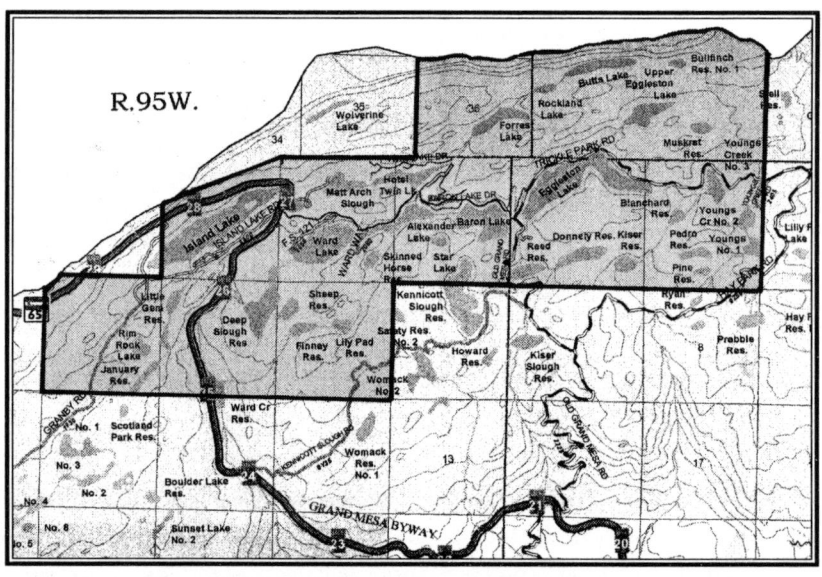

Map showing the extent of the Radcliffe preserve on Grand Mesa, covering 7040 ~~1,740~~ acres, of which he owned outright only 162 acres. This acreage was identified as part of the "private preserve" license obtained by Radcliffe in 1899.

Credit: Author

CHAPTER 13: Fishing Laws Change Again in 1899

estate under the lakes. The law also provided that Radcliffe could harvest and sell fish from his lakes in or out of season for a period of 10 years. The irony—not lost on any angler of the time—was that Radcliffe could take as much fish as he wanted from his lakes under protection from the state at any time, while others were not even allowed to have fish in their possession, out of season. Radcliffe had secured a lease from the state and also had the lease from the Alexander and Forrest company. These two leases constituted his authority to the property.

Radcliffe had an agreement with the United States Fish Commission that provided that Superintendant E.A. Tulian[18] and three men would collect eggs at the lakes, with one or two men to be at the lakes from about May 20 to June 5, then from June 5 to July 4, Tulian and three other men would remain at the lakes. From the close of the spawning season—about July 4—two men were to be left as long as possible at the lakes to monitor the hatching of the eggs and then plant the fry in the lakes. Radcliffe was to keep half of the eggs to hatch in his hatchery, and the other half were to be taken to the Leadville station for hatching. Of these, Radcliffe would get back a third of the fry for placement in his lakes.

It was an agreement that benefited both the Grand Mesa lakes as well as the State of Colorado, since the Leadville hatchery did not have the capacity to supply the entire state with fry or fingerlings.

The SCD&RC stockholders were up in arms when they learned of the exclusive fishing privilege granted Radcliffe, claiming the state constitution and their bylaws gave the board of directors no authority to sign away their rights. They resented the Britisher's lordly manner and refused to recognize his title through making application to him for personal fishing permits. They said they would fish whenever and wherever they pleased, and proceeded to prove it.

In addition to the SCD&RC stockholders, Radcliffe and his fishing rules were the talk of the county, resulting in more than a few meetings of Delta citizens to discuss the fishing privilege question at Alexander Lakes. The conclusion of these meetings was to test the law in the courts. Delta County citizens felt the fish in the public waters of the state should belong to the people of the state.

MURDER AND MYSTERY ON GRAND MESA

In June 1899, a group of Delta County citizens submitted a petition to Fish Commissioner T.H. Johnson to revoke Radcliffe's license, issued to him on May 4, 1899. In the petition, allegations of fraud and misrepresentation were made, but no evidence was ever produced to sustain the charges. The attorney for the petitioners also claimed that the Surface Creek Ditch and Reservoir Company, from whom Radcliffe leased his lakes, may, at certain seasons, use all the water that it stored in the lakes, and when a lake was void of water, the license was void, as well. The claim was that a license could only be issued when the reservoir company has water stored year round.

If the reservoir company were to take all of the stored water in a given lake, all rights to the fish in that lake would be lost (and so would the fish). Under the law, the "fishing right" attached to the "water right" and not to the water itself.

The petitioners alleged that they had secured approval, by signature, of 98 percent of the county. At a formal hearing soon after, it was stated that the people who signed the petition were, in most cases, informed of its contents by the circulators, but the paper to which the signatures were attached was an agreement to agree to the terms of the lengthy petition. When the signatures on the petition were checked, only 225 names were counted, while it was stated that the population of the county was 5,600.

Petitioners had also questioned whether the Surface Creek Ditch and Reservoir Company had clear title to the lakes when they transferred their title to Radcliffe. It was all determined to be legal.

Failing to accomplish their purpose by petition, a group of Delta County citizens filed suit in August 1899, questioning the legality of Radcliffe's Class A license. Attorney D.C. Beaman assisted Radcliffe in the suit defense and, once again, the license was determined to be legal, further irritating many county residents.

By September 1899, William Radcliffe's fish hatchery operation was reporting a capability of about 3,000,000 fry a season, with an estimated value of $100,000, according to Mr. Bloomfield, a state hatchery employee who worked at the Radcliffe hatchery. He also explained that the headwaters and lakes contiguous to such headwaters are the natural spawning ground of the trout.

CHAPTER 13: Fishing Laws Change Again in 1899

When the fish are allowed to spawn naturally in the streams, only about one-half of 1 percent of the eggs survive. In a hatchery operation, the figure is closer to 90 percent.

Radcliffe's legal issues did not end with the ruling of the courts regarding the validity of his 1899 license. At least three times in 1900, Radcliffe appeared in the county courts, first on June 18 (People vs. Radcliffe), then on July 14 (Greenwood vs. Radcliffe), and finally on September 4 (Obert & Fuller vs. Radcliffe & Puchert). On each of these occasions, the decision was to favor Radcliffe.

CHAPTER 14

Radcliffe Makes Improvements to the Resort

In 1899, Radcliffe also erected additional cabins for use by his friends from England and for his employees, and he built what some described as "an elaborate lodge" for himself. A painting of a lady of much beauty had a place of honor in his residence, though it was never revealed who she was or her importance to him. His lodge may have included hunting trophies, as well, but they most certainly were not obtained from around the world

Radcliffe's private residence at his resort on Grand Mesa. This photo originally appeared in the Denver Post, and may have been taken within a few days of the killing of William Womack.
Photo credit: Denver Public Library, Western History Department

CHAPTER 14: Radcliffe Makes Improvements to the Resort

Radcliffe Hotel. This is either the first or second photo showing the Radcliffe improvements to the exterior; the hitching post in front of the porch, the handrails on each side of the stairs, the slab side wall under the lower porch, and the removal of the remnants of the curtain over the upper porch. This photo shows six adult women, four young girls, and one small boy.

Photo credit: Delta County Historical Society

and shipped there. He had no need to attest to his skill as a hunter with such trophies. Whether he also had first editions and rare volumes on the open shelves in his library (as some reported) was debatable, as it is unlikely that his residence even contained a library. A photo of his residence appeared in a July 1901 Denver newspaper and it appeared to be a simple log cabin. Pride in his "estate" was shown by the thousands of dollars spent in building roads and driveways and in generally improving the property.

By now, his fish hatchery, on which Radcliffe claimed to have spent $15,000, had a capacity for millions, and the propagation of trout on a big scale was started. Heretofore, natural reproduction combined with the smaller Alexander-Forrest hatchery had been ample to keep the lakes fully stocked under the very limited demands upon them, due to their inaccessibility, and extensive hatchery operations had not been necessary. But now the United States Bureau of Fisheries entered into an agreement with Radcliffe, whereby it stocked the lakes with trout and returned approximately 25 percent of the harvest, which the very first year was 1,727,000 eggs. There were no refrigerator cars then as we know them, and his plan was to ship the live trout in tanks to Eastern cities or pack them in ice. It was not long before he was shipping fish by the hundreds of pounds nearly every day of the warmer months of the year via the stage from Cedaredge to Delta. From Delta, the fish were shipped by train.

From all appearances, Radcliffe's fish and game preserve was operating profitably and according to his plan. Unfortunately, one of his deputy game wardens was soon to affect his life in a way he could never imagine.

CHAPTER 15

Who Was Frank A. Mahany?

Though Frank Albert Mahany[19] was often described as a half-breed Indian in past writings of the incident described in this book, nothing is known of his Indian heritage, if he had any at all. It is believed that the "half-breed" tag was the result of mob chatter following the killing described herein. What better excuse to hang a killer than to identify him as part Indian, especially in those times? The reference to "half-breed" as a descriptor of Mahany also appeared in *The Denver Republican* of Wednesday, July 17, 1901, and was apparently quoted from a Delta source.

His father, Jeremiah, was born in New Brunswick, Canada, while his mother, Sarah, was born in New York. Jeremiah was in the mining business in Georgetown, Colorado, and had formed the Mahany Gold Mining Company[20] in July 1876. Frank was born April 5, 1865, in Georgetown, the oldest of two children. Frank also had a bit of Irish blood in his genes, as his paternal grandfather was from County Cork,[21] Ireland. It may have been Frank's Irish side that led to his temper and the shooting of a Surface Creek cattleman in 1901.

On October 27, 1887, Frank Mahany married Annie Jane Brown in Mesa County, Colorado. They had met in Fruita, Colorado, where both were living at the time of their marriage. Their first child, Paul, was born in December 1892, followed by Ralph in December 1894 and two years later, on November 28, 1896, twin girls—Mary Ethel and Sarah Esther—arrived.

Contrary to the impression received from most prior historic renderings of the 1901 shooting, Frank Mahany had only worked for William Radcliffe for six weeks, even though he had known Radcliffe for about three years. Mahany was appointed as a Deputy Game Warden by Colorado Game and Fish Commissioner, C.W. Harris, on April 4, 1901, and his commission, by its terms, was to expire on February 1, 1903. Mahany was hired by William Radcliffe on June 1, 1901. Prior to being employed as a Deputy Game Warden, he had worked on Grand Mesa for the Battlement Mesa Forest Reserve.

When William Kreutzer was appointed as the first forest ranger in the United States, his assignment eventually took him

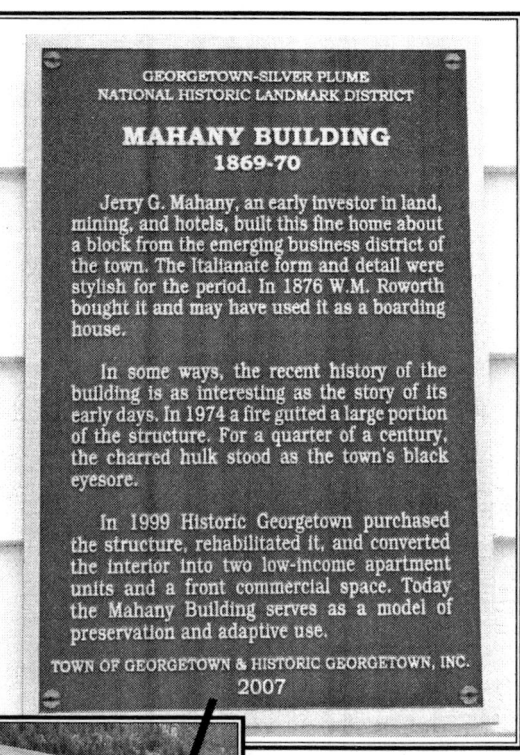

The Mahany Building in Georgetown, Colorado, where Frank A. Mahany lived as a child. The building was built by his father, Jeremiah, and was completely restored in 1999. It now houses two low-income apartment units and a commercial business.
Photo credit: Author

CHAPTER 16: Who Was Frank A. Mahany?

The marriage certificate of Frank A. Mahany and Annie Brown. They were married on October 27, 1887.

Credit: Mesa County Clerk and Recorder Office

from Colorado's Front Range (east of the Rockies) to a new assignment, by transfer, to the Battlement Mesa Forest Reserve in May 1901. The Battlement Mesa Forest Reserve, which included the Grand Mesa forests, had been the ninth reserve established by President Benjamin Harrison and was officially created in 1892. Kreutzer was told to report to Supervisor O.T. Curtis at De Beque. O.T. Curtis was supervisor of the White River Forest Reserve, but at that time, he also temporarily ran forest affairs on Battlement Mesa.

Curtis subsequently named the town of Mesa as his headquarters. Mahany had been employed by O.T. Curtis as a General Land Office fire ranger and state game warden within the Battlement Mesa Forest Reserve, and had been working in that capacity for several years before being hired by William Radcliffe in June 1901. Still technically a government employee, Mahany's salary was paid by Radcliffe, so he was considered an employee of Radcliffe and was subject to Radcliffe's direction.

While this might seem an odd situation, it should be noted that the 160-plus acres owned by Radcliffe, as well as the adjacent 160 acres owned by the Grand Mesa Resort Company, were grandfathered as private property (and still are), completely surrounded by government-owned forest, as the Alexander preemption claim (1889) and the Cockreham premption claim (1892) preceded the formation of the Forest Reserve in 1892.

Sometime during the summer of 1900, while working with the Battlement Mesa Forest Reserve, Frank Mahany had an encounter with Jefferson Reed, and it did not turn out very well for Mahany. Reed was a ditch rider for the Surface Creek Ditch and Reservoir Company and lived in a cabin not far from the Radcliffe hotel.

Jeff Reed had a bunch of men working on a reservoir east of the hotel, presumably one of SCD&RC's reservoirs, and he was camped there in a tent. Reed came in from the reservoir about 11 a.m. to stir up their cooking fires, as some of the men had beef and beans cooking for their noon meal. He went down to the creek to get some water and Frank Mahany came down there to tell him, "You'll have to put them fires out." Reed said, "No, I don't think so!" Mahany said, "Well, I know so, or I'll tell you you're going to get in trouble here. You better put the fires out, 'cause if you don't, I'll put them out." He had a pistol on his saddle, strapped on loosely, and pulled it half out of the holster. Reed just turned and went back up to his tent, which was fairly close by. His son, Leon, just a boy, was standing near Mahany when this exchange took place. Reed went into the tent, emerged with a rifle, and ran back to the creek, where Mahany was now standing next to his horse with his pistol still half in the holster. Reed said, "Now I'm tellin' you, you better get out of here or *you're* going to get in trouble. I ain't puttin' those fires out!" As Mahany started to pull his pistol out of its holster, Reed hit him aside his head with his rifle, knocking him to the ground, unconscious. He sent his son, Leon, to the creek to get a bucket of water, which he poured on Mahany's head to wash the blood from the wound created by the rifle strike. As Mahany came to and his head cleared, Reed helped him mount his horse and then told him, "Now you go on off the trail there and I won't shoot you in the back, but if you turn around and face me," he said, "I'll shoot you." So Mahany went up the trail and never did look back.

Mahany apparently did not offer any explanation as to why the cooking fires must be extinguished. However, he was

CHAPTER 16: Who Was Frank A. Mahany?

aware of the Forest Reserve law[22] regarding campfires that were unattended and was simply exercising his authority under the circumstances.

This particular incident was never made public but was told to local historians years later by Leon Reed who, as noted above, was a young boy at the time. The accuracy of the details may not be that significant, but it was widely known that, from this time forward, Frank Mahany wore a pistol sidearm and continued the practice even later when he began to work for William Radcliffe.

Radcliffe hired Frank Mahany upon the recommendation of a number of Delta citizens, whereupon a petition supposedly was submitted to Radcliffe recommending him. Radcliffe made this claim after the shooting, when he was in a meeting with Governor Orman a few days later. Somehow, the logic of this "petition" escapes me. It was unlikely that any "angler" would support a petition to hire any game warden on the mesa, since the game wardens were restricting the customary fishing practices of many fishermen trying to feed their families.

Mahany was most likely assigned to patrol Island Lake and possibly nearby Deep Ward Lake, since he had been provided a cabin not far from the dam at Island Lake. His wife, Annie, had joined him on the mesa along with his sons, Paul and Ralph, and his twin girls, Ethel and Esther. At the time of the shooting, Paul was eight years old, Ralph was six, and the twin girls were age four.

Radcliffe was very careful to instruct his wardens as to their responsibilities and what he expected of them. His instructions did not include the use of deadly power. He told them that if the person who was seen to be fishing illegally was known to them, he should first be warned away. If he refused to go, it was the duty of the warden to get another warden, so there could be a witness and no question about the evidence, and then if the intruder yet remained, they were to get a warrant for his arrest and prosecute the case. In case the poacher was unknown to them and refused to leave, the warden was to stay with him and follow him to his home, wherever that might be, where his name could be learned and steps then taken to prosecute him.

Radcliffe considered these instructions to be ironclad, and they were designed to cover just such a case that was about to unfold. The officers of the United States Fish Commission at the lake were also briefed on his instructions.

On the day of the shooting, Frank Mahany had followed these instructions to the letter, except that his frustration with uncooperative citizens and, perhaps, a bit of his Irish temper, got the best of him. He "snapped" in a way that even startled him, and it was to affect him the rest of his life.

CHAPTER 16

A Good Day for Fishing

Sunday, July 14, 1901, was a pristine day on the mesa. The sun was shining, the weather was inviting, and William Womack decided to give his hired hands a day off. Womack's ranch hands were young but hard workers, consisting of Frank L. Trickel, age 18; cousins George and Ray Gipe, both age 17; and Frank Hinchman, age 22. They had been on the mesa for the purpose of working on the dam of a storage reservoir owned by Womack in the Kennicott Park area and were enjoying a Sunday's rest. For the two Gipe cousins, this was their first trip to the mesa, as they had recently arrived from the East for a visit to relatives in the Surface Creek area.

The group headed over to the dam at Deep Ward Lake where they were joined by Sam Milton, a friend and neighbor of Womack and a deputy water master, as well. At about 2 p.m., Frank Mahany, one of Radcliffe's six game wardens, rode up to the group and, addressing Frank Trickel, asked him if he had a permit to fish. Trickel replied, "No, I'm not fishing."

He then turned to Frank Hinchman and asked him if he had a permit to fish. Hinchman told him, "Yes." He said, "Let me see it." Frank Hinchman said, "I don't know whether I have to show you my permit." Mahany said, "That is what the law requires. Show me your permit." Hinchman said, "Oh go on. Shut up your mouth." Then Mahany went away from Hinchman and went over to Womack. He asked Womack if he had a permit. Womack said, "Yes." Mahany said, "Let me see it." Womack said, "All the permit I have got is that I am a stockholder in the ditch." Mahany said, "They have passed a law this spring that all the stockholders in the Surface Creek Ditch and Reservoir Company must have a permit from Radcliffe before they can fish." Womack said, "I don't know anything about that; they haven't notified me and I will fish until they do. If I haven't got any right to fish, go down and have me arrested and we'll find out whether I have or not." Mahany made no reply, but wheeled his horse around and rode off toward the hotel.

During this encounter, Mahany kept referring to the "law" and implying that the requirement for a fishing permit was part of that law. It may have been (and was) Radcliffe's law, but it was not part of the 1899 state statutes which created private fish and game preserves. Radcliffe's insistence on fishing by permit was his way of exercising tight control over who could fish in his lakes and which lakes they could fish in.

Upon reaching the hotel, Mahany sent Deputy Game Warden Wintersteen and another man, also a deputy game warden, to arrest Womack at Deep Ward Lake, as he assumed the group would still be there and he didn't want to arrest him himself. Unfortunately, the group had departed Deep Ward Lake for Island Lake, probably expecting to fish there without interference. As soon as he had dispatched the two other deputies, Mahany started back to his home at Island Lake.

Sam Milton left the group and the rest then left for Island Lake. About halfway from Deep Ward to Island Lake, Frank Mahany caught up with them and followed them over to the lake near the dam. It was now about 3 p.m. Mahany tied his horse close to his cabin and the group went down to the dam and outlet of the lake. Mahany ran down along the dam, an angry look on his face. Womack then said to Mahany, "Will the fish bite in here, Frank?" Mahany responded, "I don't know, I haven't tried it." Mahany then turned to Frank Hinchman and said, "Hinchman, don't you throw your line in that lake. I notify all of you not to fish in that lake unless you have got a permit." Then Hinchman said to Mahany, "I thought I told you to shut your mouth," upon which Womack said to Hinchman, "That's right, Frank, stay with him. I'll see that he don't hurt you."

Womack then dismounted from his horse, placing his horse between him and Mahany, when Mahany quickly unholstered his .38 caliber Colt revolver and shot blindly toward Womack. The first shot lodged in the back of his saddle and Womack's horse

CHAPTER 16: A Good Day for Fishing

jumped away, leaving Womack exposed. Mahany fired four more shots in rapid succession. It was difficult to tell exactly who he was shooting at, but in the fusillade of bullets, he hit Womack first in the buttock, the bullet passing from the left through the right, leaving four gaping wounds from one bullet. Two of the shots were apparently directed toward Frank Hinchman, one missing him and the other hitting him in the fleshy area of his thigh, making a painful but not a dangerous wound. As Mahany was firing at Hinchman, Womack quickly mounted his horse and was attempting to get away when the sixth bullet hit him in the left side, passing through both lungs and lodging in the muscles near his tenth rib on the right side. Womack fell from his horse mortally wounded as Hinchman was spurring his horse to get away from the flying bullets. As quickly as he could, he rode the two miles over to the campsite where Womack's wife, Eliza, and her two daughters—Lydia, age 16, and Minnie, age 14—were awaiting the group's return from their fishing venture. Eliza probably tended briefly to Frank Hinchman's wound before he proceeded down the mountain for additional medical attention, and then she hastily rode to be with her dying husband.

The Gipe boys and Frank Trickel were about 20 feet away when the shooting started, but they were not in the line of fire. They were about to leave when the shooting stopped. After a short pause, Mahany said, "You sons of bitches, if you don't go and tend to the old man, I'll kill the last one of you!"

The three boys then dismounted from their horses and carried Womack into a nearby tent and placed him on a cot. The tent was normally used as a shelter for the game warden who had charge of Island Lake at that point. Hearing the shots, Deputy Game Warden Wintersteen and his partner rushed over to the dam where Womack was being tended to.

Not knowing that Frank Hinchman had ridden to alert Womack's wife, Frank Trickel set out immediately, after placing Womack in the tent, to find Womack's wife and notify her of the shooting. When he arrived and found Hinchman already there, he continued on to Cedaredge to notify a doctor and the county sheriff. Cedaredge had a new phone line to Delta and he was able to get his message to Drs. L.A. Hick and Miller in Delta and to notify Sheriff George Smith, as well. When he was able,

Hinchman also rode to Cedaredge to seek medical attention from Dr. Fairfield.

Womack's wife and the two girls soon arrived and, for the next six to seven hours, administered whatever comfort she was able to her husband. While Frank Trickel had summoned a doctor from Delta, the time required to travel from Delta to Island Lake was too long to do any good. Before the two doctors arrived, William A. Womack died about eleven o'clock that night, lying in a tent near the Island Lake dam, about eight hours after being shot.

The day after the shooting, a coroner's inquest was held at the Womack ranch in Eckert, where the sequence of events and dialogue previously described was made a matter of record by those present during the entire event. In addition to those present at the shooting, several other people were questioned regarding Womack and his prior contacts on the mesa by Radcliffe or his employees. One such Radcliffe employee, a man named

Subpoena issued by Sheriff George Smith for the July 15, 1901 coroner's inquest of William A. Womack.
Credit: Art & Gwen (a descendant of George Smith) Cannon

CHAPTER 16: A Good Day for Fishing

H.C. Getty, stated that in a recent meeting two weeks earlier with Radcliffe in his office, Radcliffe had said that Womack was a bad man and that he wished...him out of the country.

Testimony was also taken from Jefferson B. Reed of Eckert who was employed as a ditch rider and had frequent contact with William Radcliffe. Reed stated that two years earlier, in one of many conversations he'd had with Radcliffe, that Radcliffe told him if he caught Womack fishing illegally so Radcliffe could convict him, he would give him $50. "He has told me several times that Womack should be kicked off those headgates and drowned," stated Reed.

When the coroner's inquest was concluded, the verdict stated, "...William A. Womack came to his death by a gun shot, held in the hands of Frank Mahany on the 14th day of July, 1901. Said shooting was done with the intent to kill and was done feloniously without any cause or provocation." One might argue the "provocation" statement, but the jury was clearly partial to William A. Womack.

Womack's death was to trigger a series of events that would culminate in the threat of an international incident.

CHAPTER 17

Mahany Turns Himself In

Frank Mahany lived with his family in a cabin at Island Lake not too far from the dam where the shooting occurred. With the other game wardens at his side, Mahany sat out in front of his cabin with a blazing fire to silhouette the men and their rifles, a message clearly intended for those in sight of them not to attempt anything.

When the reality of what he had done hit Mahany, he probably discussed his options with his family and the other game wardens. Mahany knew he had killed an unarmed man—or one armed only with a light fishing pole, at best. He also knew that with all of the witnesses to the shooting, he would stand little chance of a self-defense plea (though in the ensuing trial, that is exactly what he did). Finally, he knew Womack had many friends, and he was worried that "Western justice" might find him swinging from the end of a rope before he could be protected by the law.

Sometime that evening, he was visited by James R. Lamar, a Justice of the Peace and friend of William Radcliffe. Mahany told him the story of the earlier events and said he hated to shoot Womack, but he had to. He had strict orders not to let anyone fish at that lake. He was stationed there to keep everyone from fishing there and he had to enforce the law.

Upon discussing the situation, Mahany, encouraged by James Lamar, decided his best option was to turn himself in to the sheriff in Delta and hope for protection under the law. So sometime between three and four o'clock in the morning, Frank Mahany set out on horseback to Delta, accompanied by James Lamar, following a seldom-used trail and covering the 40 miles in a little over four hours. He immediately gave himself up to

CHAPTER 17: Mahany Turns Himself In

Sheriff George Smith (left) and his brother Tom. Tom Smith was the deputy who took charge of Frank Mahany when he turned himself in after he killed William Womack.

Photo credit: Delta County Historical Society

Sheriff George Smith, who turned him over to his deputies, Tom Smith and Charley Owens. Sheriff Smith, along with Coroner S.B. Houts and District Attorney Millard Fairlamb, left for the scene of the murder at once.

Lamar kept secret, for many years, the fact that he had led Mahany to Delta to seek the relative safety afforded by the law. He, too, was afraid of how such news would be handled by Womack's friends. Word spread quickly throughout the Surface Creek Valley and Delta, and everybody seemed to be thoroughly incensed at the killing of Womack by one of Radcliffe's game wardens, especially when so many other anglers had also fished without permits. It didn't take long for a mob of about 25 men to gather and ride to the Mahany cabin at Island Lake, looking for the murderer of their friend, William Womack, but Mahany was enroute to Delta on a different trail, and the mob returned empty-handed.

Mahany was placed under heavy guard that Monday, as it was feared all day that some effort would be made to take him and administer quick justice, Western style. During the day, he was locked in the jury room on the second floor of the courthouse, and not in the sheriff's office or the jail cell next to it in the basement. That would be the obvious place to look.

That Monday afternoon, the two deputies attempted to make the citizens believe that Mahany had been placed on the noon train to Gunnison to be put in jail there, but the public discovered the ruse later in the day. A number of horsemen had been observed gathering in Delta and, believing that Mahany was secreted somewhere in the courthouse, four men kept a continuous surveillance of the building. Working in pairs, and beginning on opposite sides of the building, each pair would circle the building in opposite directions, passing each other twice every circle of the building. The deputies, fearing that they might be overpowered, decided to take Mahany to a safer hiding place. A trial was being conducted in the county courtroom that evening, and while it was still in progress, at about nine o'clock, Deputy Owens took the prisoner down the back stairs. At the same time, Deputy Smith arranged a distraction outside, and while the four men watching the building were off balance, Deputy Owens rushed Mahany outside in some sort of disguise and over to a

CHAPTER 17: Mahany Turns Himself In

waiting wagon and team of horses, and they immediately drove, unnoticed, to the Smith ranch about two miles south of town.

About 11 p.m., a mob of close to 100 heavily armed men stormed the courthouse when the trial had concluded, and proceeded to break into every locked door in the courthouse searching for the prisoner. Failing to find him, they searched everywhere in town where they thought it likely he could be hiding, but to no avail. They even searched the Smith ranch, expecting that Sheriff Smith might be hiding him there, but the large ranch offered a secure hiding place, and Mahany was not discovered. They kept up their search until about 4 a.m. Tuesday morning, and not finding Mahany, the crowd dispersed.

At 10 a.m. that morning, Deputies Smith and Owens hitched a buggy and drove Mahany to Olathe where, with the prisoner, they boarded the 12:20 p.m. eastbound train headed for Gunnison, where he was to be held in the Gunnison County jail until the excitement in Delta County subsided.

The *Rocky Mountain News* reported two days later: "While at the Montrose depot yesterday waiting for the train to leave for the east, Mahaney [*sic*] begged of the deputies to place him in jail at that place, as he had recognized two of the boys who had just arrived from Ouray as sons of the man who was killed, and no doubt Mahaney [*sic*] imagined that his life might be shortened a few days should they feel disposed to let it be known who he was." However, Mahany never returned to Delta as a prisoner, as he was to be tried in Gunnison under a change-of-venue order.

Word finally reached the men looking for Mahany that he was on his way to Gunnison by train and, thus, he was out of reach for now. They then turned their attention to Radcliffe and the property at the resort and started to move in that direction.

CHAPTER 18

Mob Heads for the Lakes

L.L. Wintersteen was on the payroll of William Radcliffe when the killing of William Womack occurred on the fourteenth of July. Wintersteen was actually employed by the Fish and Game Commission out of Leadville, but he worked at Radcliffe's fish hatchery in that capacity and as a Deputy Game Warden. When he headed down the hill on the afternoon of the sixteenth, he was transporting a load of fish for shipment on the stage to Delta, which was due in Cedaredge that evening. He stopped within a

Radcliffe Hotel. This photo also shows the exterior improvements made by Radcliffe; It is the only photo without any people in it, and suggests it may have been taken before the season opened in June or after the season closed. This is the last photo in the sequence of five and may have been taken closer to 1901.

Photo credit: Delta County Historical Society

CHAPTER 18: Mob Heads for the Lakes

quarter mile of the store and post office, planning to camp overnight following his delivery of the fish to the stage driver. After supper, Wintersteen walked toward the post office, and when he was a short distance from the store, he saw a large crowd of men and boys, some making loud talk. On passing by, he heard the names Radcliffe and Puchert mentioned, and one saying he wished they were both there, as he would hang them both.

On reaching the store, there were even more men inside, seemingly quite agitated. He noticed a friend of his, who told him that the crowd was gathering to go up to the lakes and destroy Radcliffe's property, but they had agreed not to harm any of his employees if they would leave the property at once.

When the stage drove up, Wintersteen heard someone giving orders to the driver not to carry any more fish, for they were not going to allow any more to be shipped under any circumstances. Seeing it was useless to try to talk the driver into carrying his fish shipment, Wintersteen promptly returned to his camp, saddled his horse, and rode in haste back to the lakes.

On his return to the lakes, at about 7 p.m., Wintersteen first stopped at a cabin owned by J.C. Gale, and which that night was occupied by Gale, Sheriff George Smith, Mr. Lamar, and one of the Gipe boys. Sheriff Smith had been summoned to the mesa following the killing of Womack and was still investigating the murder. When Wintersteen informed the sheriff that a mob was forming in Cedaredge[23] to burn the Radcliffe buildings, Sheriff Smith dismissed the notion and basically ignored the warning.

Wintersteen's report could not have been much of a surprise, because *The Denver Republican* had even reported on Tuesday that "there will be further trouble at the lakes tonight, as a posse of about 50 men are reported to be headed for Grand Mesa."

Closer to Delta, *The Daily Sentinel* of Grand Junction even reported on Tuesday: "He [Radcliffe] is now in Denver at the Brown Palace hotel. There are rumors about Delta this morning that the friends of Womack, the dead man, will attempt to destroy Radcliffe's property, including the fish hatcheries, on which there has been spent a great deal of money."

On arriving back at the hotel, Wintersteen awoke Commissioner Henry J. Puchert and told him there was a mob on the way to burn the buildings. In haste, the two men awoke their women and children, those staying as guests at the hotel, and Commissioner Edward M. Ball, and told them to quickly pack their personal possessions. They had just about finished their packing when the first of the mob arrived. It was about 12:30 a.m. the morning of Wednesday, July 17.

It didn't take the mob long to realize that Radcliffe was not at the resort. Their thirst for a hanging was not to be realized that night, but the younger members of the mob—one waving a bloodied shirt supposedly belonging to William Womack—raised a new cry, this time to set fire to the buildings.

The leader, speaking to Wintersteen, Puchert, and Ball, ordered them to remove their personal effects from the buildings; that they were taking possession of the buildings and that there may be a fire. That was an understatement!

In a statement Henry J. Puchert made under oath about 10 days later, he stated that he had heard Jeff Reed (one of the masked mob), whose voice he recognized, say, "If Mr. Radcliffe were present he might be hung or made away with in some fashion." Even Sheriff Smith was heard to say later, "It was a mighty good thing for Mr. Radcliffe he was not there, or he, Mr. Radcliffe, might have been lynched instead of Mahany."[24]

The hotel was the largest structure, and was the first target of the mob. Inside the hotel, a second-floor balcony overlooked the front hallway entrance, and the men carried the furnishings and furniture out of the four upstairs rooms and threw them off the balcony, creating a large mound of furniture below. As soon as they had everything piled up below the balcony, someone said, "Are you ready?" They said, "Yes," and a man with a kerosene lamp threw it into the furniture and away it went. Everybody rushed out of the lodge in a hurry as the building, made entirely of lumber and logs, eagerly took to the flames.

One of the men in the mob involved in the burning of the hotel had a very large, gentle dog that followed around after the men, and no one paid much attention to him. When the dog turned up missing after the fire, it was assumed that it had inadvertently been closed into a room. The dog was the only fatality of the evening.

The fires on Grand Mesa that night were seen by hundreds throughout the Surface Creek Valley, all the way into Delta, and

CHAPTER 18: Mob Heads for the Lakes

east to Hotchkiss and beyond. The mob spared no building that they thought belonged to Radcliffe. They set fire to the hotel, Radcliffe's residence and everything in it, two rental cabins, two outhouses, the stable, which was large enough to hold 12 horses and 10 tons of hay, and the fencing and gates for four pastures.

In Radcliffe's cabin, the cry changed again to "Get Radcliffe!" and one of the men grabbed a portrait of the beautiful lady[25] hanging in a place of honor, and proceeded to shred the canvas with his knife and brake it's frame to bits, an act demonstrating the emotion of the moment. In the next minute, flames were licking all of Radcliffe's furnishings, leaping up the walls and consuming the entire building.

Down the hill from Radcliffe's cabin stood the fish hatchery on the shore of Alexander Lake. The leader of the mob asked the three men (Puchert, Ball, and Wintersteen) who worked for the government, and he was informed that the three of them were employed by the Colorado Fish and Game Commission. Then the mob leader asked them what property there belonged to the government, and he was told that the fish hatchery, along with eight cans[26] and a pair of boots, belonged to the state, whereupon they retrieved all of the cans (four were in the area of the hotel) and the boots and, led by Ball, the mob leader walked down the hill to the hatchery and placed the cans and boots inside the hatchery, and declared to Ball that they would be cared for—meaning the hatchery and items within would not be destroyed that night. In that moment, they believed the hatchery building was government owned.

For a hundred years or better, this story had a different, much more colorful version, and it was based on an article in *The Denver Republican* of Friday, July 19, 1901, which stated that as the mob started toward the fish hatchery, the employees of the Colorado Fish and Game Commission saw the approaching torches and were turning to each other in despair when one grabbed an American flag and quickly hung it in front of the building. It reportedly unfurled and waved gently in the breeze just as the lead members of the mob reached the hatchery, and as the flag symbolized the government, the men turned and went back to the cottages to watch them burn to the ground. It is not likely that there was an American flag anywhere within 20 miles of the mesa, though the story did add a different touch of emotion to the event, notwithstanding the fact that the mob displayed not a whit of patriotism, but simply did not wish to antagonize the state government. The murder of Womack was a local issue, and the mob leaders wished it to remain such.

As Wintersteen, Puchert, and Ball loaded their possessions into a wagon, they had to inform the mob leader that their team for the wagon could not be obtained till morning, since the horses were somewhere in the pasture, so several men offered to help them pull the wagon to a safe place out of danger from the fire. They pulled the wagon about 300 yards to a spot about 10 yards from the Gale cabin. J.C. Gale was the man who had built the hotel about 10 years earlier. At this time, the men in the cabin, including the sheriff, were "asleep."

By this time, it was about 2 a.m. Wintersteen and the others proceeded to arouse the men in the cabin and told the sheriff that they had been ordered away from the hill by an armed and masked mob numbering from 75 to 100 men. The sheriff and others seemed surprised, as they claimed to have heard nothing, although the mob had ridden within about eight yards of the cabin, and many shots were fired into the air near the hotel, not far from the cabin where the men had been "sleeping." Sheriff Smith and Mr. Gale quickly dressed and started toward the hotel and returned almost immediately, saying that three bullets had passed uncomfortably near them and it would be very risky to try to proceed further. During the fire, and for some time after, the mob indulged in reckless shooting. As the fires died down, the mob formed a cordon of mounted men between Delta and the Grand Mesa to watch for Radcliffe.

When daylight arrived, Wintersteen, Puchert, and Ball returned to the hotel to find Radcliffe's private dwelling, the two-story hotel, two cabins, the stable, and the contents of all, burned to the ground. Only the fish hatchery and ice house remained intact.

Following the Womack killing and the burning of the resort buildings, the lake holdings of Radcliffe were considered open fishing for all. When L.L. Wintersteen returned to the area about two weeks later, he found no fewer than 100 people at Alexander Lake, most fishing with hook and line. However, they

CHAPTER 18: Mob Heads for the Lakes

were taking everything that would bite, whether big or small. It was stock-up time for Delta County fishermen, and on some days, there were reported to be 150 people fishing, with no concern regarding limit. It was estimated that well over 200 pounds of fish were caught every day by the anglers for the next 30 days. The word was out that there was open fishing in the Radcliffe lakes. Oddly enough, however, the "mob" insisted that only legal (hook and line) fishing would be permitted, and that they would hang anyone caught fishing otherwise. However, they ignored the 20-pound legal limit per person per day.

It was popular opinion that if Radcliffe ever returned to look after his lakes, he would very quickly be swinging at the end of a rope. Henry J. Puchert communicated the situation to Radcliffe in Denver as soon as possible, and further said, "In my opinion, your life is in danger if you come on your property or anywhere in the vicinity of Delta; and in my opinion, such danger still continues."

With no one to care for the fish at the hatchery from July 16 to 29, it was estimated that over half of the young fish had died within several weeks after the fires. They figured there had been over 1,500,000 fish or eggs when all of the employees had been kicked off the hill. Radcliffe had employed from seven to eleven men receiving from $30 to $90 a month for the purpose of protecting, propagating, and selling fish. His game wardens were included as employees.

When several state and federal fish culturists did finally return to the hatchery about two weeks after the killing of Womack, they found about half of the eggs and fry dead, and much of the remaining fry diseased. Regardless, they turned them into Alexander Lake. The fish hatchery, at that point, was closed.

CHAPTER 19

Radcliffe Was Out of Town

Perhaps no part of this story has been more difficult to research than the whereabouts of William Radcliffe at the time of the murder. For much of the week after the killing of Womack, the media simply reported the fact that Radcliffe was not on the mesa or in the area. Indeed, the mob of about 100 riders searched high and low for him for two days, and their frustration in not finding him led them ultimately to harm him, in their judgment, by burning his possessions.

On Tuesday, July 16, 1901, the *Denver Post* reported, "William Radcliffe, the proprietor of the Grand Mesa lakes, is expected in Denver tomorrow," though other sources noted that Radcliffe was not even aware of the shooting until Wednesday. Then on Wednesday, the *Denver Times* stated, "Mr. Radcliffe is in Denver,..." however, he was not in Denver until Thursday, by his own statement.

With so many newspapers throughout the state of Colorado reporting on the events surrounding the killing, just what was their source of information? It is clear that there were correspondents sent to Delta County from several Denver newspapers, and at least one was in Delta from Grand Junction, Colorado.

In fact, so many newspapers were reporting on the event that some even accused others of not having correct facts, as though their version of the story was the most accurate one. No matter, they all got creative with the "facts" in order to fill in the unknown details.

This was big news—not because a man was killed, but because the killing involved an employee of William Radcliffe. Radcliffe was well known on both sides of Grand Mesa, and not well liked

CHAPTER 19: Radcliffe Was Out of Town

in either Delta or Mesa Counties. In Denver, Radcliffe associated with the elite, a completely different class of sportsmen.

In Delta County, *The Delta Independent* weekly newspaper had nothing in print until their Friday (July 19) regular issue, headlined, "MURDERED!", though many of the citizens of the county knew the story in detail on Monday, the day after the murder. By then, any employee of Radcliffe was in danger. The mob of angry citizens and friends of Womack, most of whom were from the Surface Creek area, were not out for revenge—they were out for blood! Naturally, Mahany was their prime target, but others were at risk, too.

Only one or two people actually knew William Radcliffe's destination when he departed his mesa preserve prior to Sunday, July 14. One, for sure, was Radcliffe's overseer, Jefferson Smith, and the other was probably his Delta County attorney, Alfred R. King.

Very little is known about Jeff Smith, except that he had worked for Radcliffe for several years as his foreman or overseer at the Grand Mesa preserve. Smith had family living in the Cedaredge area, suggesting that he did not actually live at the preserve, reinforced by the notation in the 1900 census that his occupation was "day laborer." He did not exercise any control over the fish hatchery operation, but he more than likely managed most elements of the resort, subject to Radcliffe's direction.

It is hard to imagine that Radcliffe would leave the mesa and not inform his foreman of his destination, so it can be assumed that Smith knew exactly where Radcliffe was on the day of the killing, yet there was no mention of him being questioned by the sheriff or by the mob when, as reported by *The Denver Republican*, he was on the mesa when the mob burned the hotel and other structures early Wednesday morning.

Did Smith make any effort on Monday or Tuesday to notify Radcliffe of the killing? He probably didn't realize until the arson event and his experience with the hostility of the mob that Radcliffe's life was in danger, should he try to return home.

There were only three news sources that really provided details of the killing of Womack and the events afterward, and all were published on Friday, July 19, 1901. The most accurate were *The Delta Independent* and *The Delta Laborer* ("IT WAS MURDER!"), both local Delta newspapers published to inform with facts without much fluff. The other, *The Denver Republican*, printed a long article filled with basic facts, lots of verbal emotion, and an abundance of misquotes and distorted details. Unfortunately, the paper was the most-quoted source used by other media at the time, and it was almost the sole source of information used by Alice Spencer Cook when she wrote two consecutive articles for *Western Sportsman* magazine in August and September 1940. Unfortunately, the Cook articles have been used time and again as authoritative sources in more contemporary writings about these events. It is no wonder that so many factual errors have corrupted this part of the story.

So, where did Radcliffe go when he left his preserve on Grand Mesa? It is quite clear from subsequent testimony by him that his destination was the Crystal River valley somewhere south of Glenwood Springs, and that would be either Carbondale or Redstone, Colorado. He could have traveled by horse and buggy to his destination, but that was not Radcliffe's style: He went by train. So he had two options: he could catch the train in Delta, a 28-mile ride by horse and buggy from his hotel on a very rough wagon road, or he could go off the mesa on the north side from his hotel and ride to De Beque—a longer ride and a worse road, but it was the closest train depot to the north. Let us assume he traveled to Delta, as his attorney, A.R. King was there and was probably consulted on business matters. Let us assume that he also left town the day before the killing. Radcliffe's actual departure was never documented in the press or elsewhere.

Therefore, let us assume that William Radcliffe left his Grand Mesa property on Saturday, July 13, 1901, by horse or buggy and rode to Delta, a trip that probably took him about five or six hours. His final destination that day was either Glenwood Springs, Carbondale, or Redstone, Colorado. He arrived in Delta in time to board the 2:35 p.m. westbound Denver & Rio Grande narrow gauge train[27] to Grand Junction, arriving about 4:40 p.m., and then boarded the eastbound D&RG at 6:35 p.m.[28] or the Colorado Midland train at 6:45 p.m., both of which went on standard gauge rails to Glenwood Springs and beyond, but only the Colorado Midland went further east by way of Carbondale.

CHAPTER 19: Radcliffe Was Out of Town

Radcliffe would not have ridden to Carbondale by horse, even though he was an excellent equestrian. A man of his assumed stature would travel in comfort, and the train was far more comfortable than horse-drawn buggy. Radcliffe was also known to be very sociable and would have chosen the train simply as an opportunity to converse with other businessmen and catch up on the news. He would have arrived in Glenwood Springs about 9:10 p.m. on Saturday and probably stayed overnight at the Hotel Colorado. He would have stayed in the best hotel in the area, and Carbondale did not offer similar accommodations, had he traveled on the Colorado Midland or changed to the Midland in Glenwood Springs.

Through Radcliffe's friend and Denver attorney, David C. Beaman, who was also the attorney and legal advisor for Colorado Fuel & Iron, John C. Osgood had purchased over 4,200 acres of land in the Crystal River valley, which would eventually encompass the village of Redstone and his new mansion, named "Cleveholm Manor." The entire property was known then as the Crystal River Ranch, and Osgood had a summer home on the estate near the new mansion under construction. It would not be long before many referred to the Osgood mansion as the "Redstone Castle." While Alice Spencer Cook, in her 1940 article, claimed that William Radcliffe visited Osgood at the new mansion on Wednesday, July 17, 1901, the mansion was still under construction, and by October 1901, it only had one story completed with just the beginning framing of the second story. Osgood was not living in the mansion; he was still living in his summer home on the ranch. The "castle" was not completed till 1902.

So, where did Radcliffe go on Sunday, the day of the killing?

On Friday, July 19, 1901, *The Denver Republican* newspaper carried a detailed article about the killing and arson, and Radcliffe, then in Denver, was quoted as saying, "I first learned of the killing down there while I was at a ranch I own in another part of the state." This quote is believed to be inaccurate, possibly a result of Radcliffe's English accent and it not being heard accurately, or it was simply a misinterpretation of his statement.

Radcliffe did not own any land in Pitkin County (Redstone area), Garfield County (Glenwood Springs and Carbondale area), or Gunnison County, based on a thorough check of county land records. However, Gunnison and Pitkin County land records show that David C. Beaman owned hundreds of acres of land in both counties. Was Radcliffe lying? I suspect that he was probably staying with and conferring with David C. Beaman, the man who was the main force behind the 1899 Colorado legislation that created private fish and game preserves and the cause of Radcliffe's problems at his resort on Grand Mesa. Radcliffe likely did not want his meeting with Beaman to become public knowledge.

Then there is the question of when Radcliffe actually visited with John C. Osgood. The day before the killing on Grand Mesa, on Saturday, July 13, Osgood was attending a Colorado Fuel & Iron Company stockholders meeting in Denver. At the time, CF&I was embroiled in issues regarding the UMWA miners union, so the meeting was likely an all-day affair. On Sunday, Osgood traveled to Pueblo to spend the day with a man named Julian Kennedy, who was believed to be interested in buying CF&I, and who was an associate of J.P. Morgan, the well-known financier. Osgood probably had traveled on his own private train, consisting of an engine and private car, and if Radcliffe was loaned that same train to get to Denver, as he noted later, then we can assume Osgood had returned to his ranch near Redstone by Wednesday.[29]

Just how did Radcliffe learn about the killing at his preserve? The *Basalt Journal* newspaper didn't carry the story until Saturday, July 20. The *Avalanche Echo*, a Glenwood Springs newspaper, carried a small article on Thursday, July 18. The *Marble Times* and the *Crystal River Lance* made no mention of it at all. And the *Glenwood Post*, the main newspaper in Glenwood Springs at the time, made no mention of the event until Saturday, July 20, well beyond the time Radcliffe had moved on to Denver.

It is possible that Osgood had seen the headlines that every newspaper in Denver had posted on Tuesday, July 16, regarding the killing. None of them agreed with the headline quoted in the Cook article.[30] The actual headlines were as follows:

Denver Post	MESA LAKE KILLER GAVE NO WARNING
Denver Times (morning)	DEPUTY GAME WARDEN SHOOTS TWO FISHERS

CHAPTER 19: Radcliffe Was Out of Town

Denver Times (afternoon)   MOB TRIES TO LYNCH!

The Denver Republican   ANGLER KILLED BY GAME WARDEN

Rocky Mountain News   MAN KILLED BY GAME WARDEN

While in Pueblo, Osgood would not have seen any mention of the Grand Mesa killing in the *Pueblo Chieftain*, as it first appeared in that primary Pueblo newspaper on Thursday, July 18, on page 9. Not exactly headline news, the article read: "FIRED IN REVENGE. GRAND MESA LAKE HOTEL WAS DESTROYED." It is fairly certain that Osgood was aware of the killing when he arrived back in Redstone, and since the D&RG rails went due west from Pueblo through Salida and then northwest to Leadville and beyond, he must have seen and obtained a Tuesday Denver newspaper while in Pueblo or enroute home. No doubt he would be curious how the CF&I stockholders meeting would be treated in the press.

We do not know if Osgood was expecting a visit from his English friend, but it is likely that the visit with he and Beaman was prearranged. As they walked into Osgood's ranch home on Wednesday, July 17, Osgood probably handed Radcliffe one of the Denver newspapers, which he might have picked up on his return from Pueblo. Up to this time, Radcliffe had no knowledge of the events that had taken place back on Grand Mesa. Ironically, at that moment, his resort buildings were probably still smoldering from fires set the previous evening, though that news had yet to appear in the press.

Radcliffe probably read the account in silence, wondering what possibly could have provoked his game warden, Frank Mahany, to go to such extremes as to kill William Womack. Secretly, he might have had a moment of understanding, since he often had similar feelings against Womack, who he considered a troublemaker. There can be no doubt that Radcliffe felt the urgency to return to his resort to see what he could do to clean up the mess, but he had also noted in the newspaper that the citizens of Delta County were after Mahany's neck as well as that of his employer, William Radcliffe.

There is little doubt that he discussed the situation with both Osgood and Beaman, probably deciding that the only safe way to return home was with an official armed escort of state troops, and that could only be provided with the authority and by order of Governor James B. Orman in Denver.

Osgood's private train was parked on a siding in Redstone, and he offered the use of his train to Radcliffe. Radcliffe reacted to the news with a sense of urgency to move on to Denver immediately and likely did not wish to wait for a scheduled train out of Carbondale. As quickly as he was able, Radcliffe set out for Denver on the one-car train over the Crystal River Railroad, which had been built from Carbondale south to Redstone and beyond.

The Osgood train circled north to Carbondale, where it switched to the Denver & Rio Grande or the Colorado Midland rail system and proceeded east to Denver. The D&RG rails to Denver went by way of Pueblo. The Colorado Midland rails went by way of Colorado Springs, so the Colorado Midland route was shorter and probably quicker.

In Radcliffe's own sworn statement to the British Embassy on December 20, 1901, he said, "I went to Denver the moment I heard of the affair, and made formal application by and with my counsel, to the governor of the state of Colorado that I be put in possession of the property and industry from which myself and employees had been driven." This statement suggests that his counsel might have ridden with him to Denver and, in this case, it would have been David C. Beaman. In fact, Beaman had probably accompanied him to Osgood's home, or they all may have met at Beaman's home.

If Jeff Smith, Radcliffe's foreman at the Grand Mesa resort, had rushed to Delta and sent telegram after telegram attempting to catch Radcliffe on his return to the lakes, to warn him not to return because a lynch mob awaited his return, as numerous writings of the event have stated, he would have assumed his employer would be traveling west by scheduled train from Carbondale to Grand Junction, etc. Radcliffe's foreman assumed all along that Radcliffe was planning to return to the Grand Mesa ranch upon completion of his visit to Beaman and Osgood. Furthermore, he had no way of knowing whether Radcliffe was aware of the situation back in Delta County.

On Friday, July 19, 1901, *The Denver Republican* newspaper carried a detailed article about the killing and arson, and Radcliffe,

CHAPTER 19: Radcliffe Was Out of Town

now in Denver, was quoted as saying, "By the kindness of John C. Osgood in furnishing me an engine and a car, I made my way to Ribston and was there warned that I must proceed no further."

The mention of "Ribston," assumed to be a station stop or some type of stop that had telegraph service available, was interesting, because a station or telegraph stop by that name did not exist. The Cook version of this story placed Ribston as the last station stop before Radcliffe's ranch, and further stated that a telegram finally reached him at that stop. It is possible that Ribston might have been a typo, as there was a station seven miles northwest of Denver called "Ralston," except that Ralston was not even close to any rail system that Radcliffe might have traveled.

It was *The Denver Republican* that same Friday that reported, rather dramatically, the following part of the story:

> *Warned by a telegram, which almost missed catching the special train on which he was traveling, William Radcliffe, member of the Denver club and gentleman farmer, narrowly escaped lynching at the hands of an angry mob this week. He fled to Denver to appeal to the governor to protect him and his property. He was too late to save his hotel and fish hatcheries, for the infuriated crowd burned them while he was on his way here. He arrived here [Denver] yesterday morning.*
>
> *While Radcliffe knew there was some feeling against him because the game warden was in his employ and was guarding his preserves, he had no thought of personal danger until he received this telegram: Don't come to the Grand Mesa; you will surely be hanged to the nearest limb. The mob will not ask a question after they are sure you are William Radcliffe.*
>
> *Completely nonplussed by the message, its emphatic language prevailed upon Radcliffe to keep away. While the message was flashing along the wire from station to station trying to overtake the train consisting of one car and an engine, mounted and armed men were searching every foot of ground in the mesa, hoping to locate either Radcliffe or Warden Mahany. So determined and diligent were they that Game Warden Harris, who went to investigate the shooting, was followed for miles because the mob wanted to make him recant an alleged interview of his in which he commended the action of Mahany.*

MURDER AND MYSTERY ON GRAND MESA

By just five minutes Radcliffe missed going to his doom. Had the telegram been sent a little later he would be hanging from a tree in the mesa, instead of enjoying the hospitality of the Denver club. His special train had reached the last telegraph station before arriving at the stop close to his ranch. Even after he received it, he was incredulous. He was inclined to go on, but if he had taken the ride that Warden Harris took and had seen horses saddled at every house and Winchesters protruding from the windows he would have realized of what serious impact the words were.

Anyone familiar with Colorado train travel in 1901 would have noted the errors and distortions in these statements. If Radcliffe was trying to return to his ranch, he would have gone west from Glenwood Springs, not east by way of Denver, Pueblo, Salida, etc. The westbound route was standard gauge track only as far as Grand Junction. The rails from Grand Junction south to Delta were narrow gauge. At Grand Junction, Radcliffe would have had to wait for a scheduled D&RG passenger train to Delta. The Osgood private train could not have proceeded beyond Grand Junction.

The eastbound route had standard gauge only as far as Salida.[31] From there, over Marshall Pass and beyond to Gunnison, Montrose, and Delta, the tracks were narrow gauge. Again, Osgood's train could not have continued past Salida, Colorado. At Salida, Radcliffe would have had to wait for a scheduled westbound D&RG passenger train to Delta.

Just how did Osgood's small train manage to share tracks with regularly scheduled trains? Osgood did not have authority to "clear the tracks," and his train would have been subject to the control of a train dispatcher in Denver or Grand Junction, and thus may have spent some time on sidings waiting for "scheduled" trains to pass.

Given the known facts of what was and was not possible regarding Radcliffe's transportation, the scenario described by *The Denver Republican* made no sense. Even the telegraph story

CHAPTER 19: Radcliffe Was Out of Town

made no sense, as a telegraph message needed to be sent only once since all stations on the circuit would get it simultaneously. Such a message would have been identified as an emergency, and all operators on the circuit would have read it. Normal telegraph communication on the railroad would have identified the intended receiver station first, and other stations on the circuit would have ignored it. Such would not have been the situation with this emergency communication.

Radcliffe's own sworn and notarized statements in December 1901 never mentioned any attempt to return to his ranch during the week after the killing, but other facts were explicit and detailed. Even after being notified of the killing, his actions confirmed that he was headed east, not west.

Osgood's private train, with Radcliffe and probably Beaman on board, clearly had Denver as its destination. While *The Denver Republican* newspaper described most of the facts of the story accurately, they simply misinterpreted or made up others. They were the only Denver newspaper that carried that version of the story.

The drama regarding the telegram that kept missing the train, station after station, made for good reading in *The Denver Republican*, but Jeff Smith, Radcliffe's foreman at the Grand Mesa lodge, knew where he was, and only had to telegraph Glenwood Springs, Carbondale, or Redstone to notify him of the danger in returning home. Furthermore, Smith had no way of knowing Radcliffe was heading for Denver and not Grand Junction-Delta, and on a one-car private train, as well. Only Osgood knew that detail. Then there was the issue that a few of the mob were at the Delta train depot waiting for Radcliffe's return, and no friend of Radcliffe would have dared even to come near the depot on that Monday or Tuesday.

Smith and all other employees of Radcliffe were kicked off the mesa the night the mob burned the hotel, Wednesday morning about 2 a.m. However, they were not permitted to exit the mesa to the south. They were sent over the north side of the mesa on the wagon road to the towns of Mesa and De Beque. Several of the hatchery employees actually lived in the Plateau Valley area, so they were simply "going home." Smith would have sent the telegram, probably sometime later Wednesday morning, from De Beque, since De Beque was a railroad station stop and had telegraph capability.

In all likelihood, it was probably John Osgood who forwarded the telegram from Jeff Smith to Radcliffe, since it was likely he had intercepted it in Redstone. Any telegram to Radcliffe could just as easily been sent by the hatchery employees who, by then, would have known Radcliffe's location.

Radcliffe was safe in Denver, but his life, from this time on, would be forever changed.

CHAPTER 20

Commissioner Harris Investigates

When Colorado Fish & Game Commissioner Charles W. Harris let it be known that he was heading for Delta and then to Grand Mesa to investigate the killing, he was told by many that it would be dangerous for him to appear on the grounds, because he had been inaccurately quoted in an afternoon Denver paper as saying that he considered the killing of Womack justifiable. The *Rocky Mountain News* had reported on Tuesday, July 16, that: "Commissioner Harris yesterday said he was quite certain that the men killed and wounded were dynamiting fish, and that McHaney [*sic*] was simply doing his duty in attempting to arrest them and killing them if necessary."

In no way daunted by this, he kept on, determined to investigate the matter thoroughly. He arrived in Delta by train from Denver and then had difficulty finding someone willing to accompany him to Cedaredge. He finally convinced the liveryman from whom he hired the team to drive the team, and they were on their way. As they proceeded from Delta, first to the home of Frank Hinchman near Cedaredge, they noticed small groups of armed horsemen along the trail whose manner and bearing did not make them feel at ease.

Upon concluding his business with Hinchman, Harris was returning at about two o'clock in the morning, still with his driver, when he was stopped by a group of armed men who, in a threatening manner, demanded to know if he was Harris, the game warden. Replying that he was the man, they then wanted to know why he had stated that Mahany was justified in killing Womack in self-defense.

"I told them," said Harris, "that I had made no such statement; that I had been misquoted." He went on to say that he knew nothing more about Mahany, but that Mahany had been recommended to him for appointment by reputable citizens of the county, and that his only knowledge of the shooting was contained in a telegram from Mahany, which stated that he had shot and killed Womack in self-defense.

"At first they were rather threatening in their manner, but they finally seemed to accept my explanations, and the leaders, suppressing the more hot blooded, then gave the word to withdraw and let me proceed." As he was leaving the group, someone shouted, "Down with Radcliffe! If we get him, we'll hang him to the biggest tree on the mesa!"

When Commissioner Harris returned to Denver, he was called to Governor Orman's office for a meeting behind locked doors. Orman was upset because he had heard that Harris had publicly said that the men who were shot got merely their just desserts. As he had stated in Delta County the day before, Harris told the governor that he had not made any statement of the sort. Harris did state, however, that he had expressed a general opinion that persons who were dynamiting fish and were caught by game wardens and who refused to desist must be ejected from preserves by force and could not complain if they were hurt if they were caught in violating the state game laws. Though Governor Orman was satisfied that Harris had not made the statement attributed to him by the Denver newspaper, the fallout from the conference was that about 150 deputy game wardens throughout Colorado were recalled and removed from office. They had been appointed by the state to watch private fish ponds and game preserves but were paid by the respective resort owners. Governor Orman was simply trying to avoid future problems with the 1899 fish and game law, and though he questioned the legality of the law, it had been in effect over two years and was widely exercised in the state. His attorney general was finally directed to study the law and make recommendations to "fix" it.

CHAPTER 21

No Protection, Says Governor

On Friday, July 19, Radcliffe met with Governor James Orman and with Fish and Game Commissioner Harris in Denver for several hours. Radcliffe argued that he was denied the right of the possession and use of his property on Grand Mesa, and that it was the duty of the state to protect him and to put him in control of his property. He went on to argue that because he provided a great many spawn to the state, that he was entitled to state protection. He also stated that he would submit a claim for damages to the state of Colorado, and if that was not satisfied, he would appeal to the English government to assist in the collection of the claim. He knew from his discussion with Harris that he could not return safely to the mesa and, for that reason, had asked the governor for protection by the state.

In his conversation with Governor Orman, Radcliffe claimed that from four to five anglers had been warned or arrested annually for the past several years for violations of the state fish and game laws. Radcliffe described Mahany as a "quiet, faithful, unemotional man—a man with a level head."

In a statement he made to a *Denver Times* reporter after the meeting, Radcliffe said, "It is not a question of whether or not I am in legal possession of the Grand Mesa lakes, but a question of whether a man can be evicted by a mob, his property destroyed and his people driven away and the state not give him any protection." Radcliffe was also quoted in the *Denver Times* as saying:

> Since 1895, no one has ever been refused a permit to fish in the lakes, provided the state laws were observed, and they were allowed to take away their whole catch. For this

reason, I have been permitted by three successive game wardens to have deputy game and fish wardens to assist in protecting the fish. ...Although four or five people were warned and arrested annually, there was never a shot fired until the other day. With the exception of Mahany, not one of the wardens employed at Grand Mesa carried a gun. Mahany did so because his life had been threatened by parties with whom he had trouble when employed policing the United States Forest Reserve. I have known him three years, though he was not employed by me until this year, and I regard him as an unemotional man who would not commit an act rashly. Mr. Curtis, supervisor of the forest reserve, will confirm this opinion of him.

The published statement that I offered Mahaney hundreds of dollars to shoot anybody is absolutely false. It may have grown out of a standing offer to my watchers of $50 for any conviction for an infringement of the state game laws. Ever since my acquisition of the lakes certain parties in Delta county have made it a practice to get their year's supply of fish by putting down the headgates of the connecting streams between the lakes, thus cutting off the water, and taking out wagon loads of fish which had ascended the stream for spawning purposes. This was in direct violation of the law and was killing the goose that laid the golden egg.

In the past five years I have spent $30,000 in improving this property, and the loss to me by having to leave the fish uncared for will be no less than $10,000. It is a business proposition with me, and I believe I have a right to ask the state to protect my property.

Indeed, William Radcliffe had suffered a huge loss. He was unable to fulfill any of his contracts for fish, fish eggs, or fry. In the previous year, he had sold 6,314 pounds of fish from June 10, 1900, through the season, and in one month of 1901, he had sold 4,106 pounds at prices from 27½ to 40 cents per pound net. Fish eggs and fry were sold at $4 to $5 per thousand.

Governor Orman directed Assistant Attorney General Merwin to investigate Radcliffe's claim for aid in securing the protection of his property. While in Delta, Merwin had a talk

CHAPTER 21: No Protection, Says Governor

with Delta County Sheriff Smith, and the sheriff promised to see that Radcliffe was not molested if he returned to the area. He explained that he would not be able to insure Radcliffe's safety if he insisted on going to the Grand Mesa, as the feeling there was still very bitter. But the governor would not send any aid to or with Radcliffe unless requested by Sheriff Smith.

By mid-August 1901, Radcliffe had decided to take his fight to Washington, D.C. Though there were still rumors that he had completed the process for United States citizenship, in fact, he had not. Radcliffe was still, technically, an English citizen. In Washington, D.C., he planned to meet with the U.S. Attorney General and to request the dispatch of United States troops to the Grand Mesa for his protection.

Radcliffe tried to hold the Fish and Game Commission in Washington, D.C. responsible for breach of contract, and the attorney general of the United States telegraphed the district attorney in Denver, ordering him to make inquiry and, if possible, to send a U.S. fish culturist or two with protection to the lakes to care for the abandoned hatcheries, thus enabling the government to fulfill its contract. The "protection" simply was not available. At the same time, friends of Radcliffe in Delta County had apparently heard that he was ready to dispose of his Colorado holdings and bid good-by to the state of Colorado and the United States.

When Commissioner Harris received a telegram two weeks later, it was revealed that Radcliffe was planning a return to Colorado, even though his efforts to secure protection from both the state and federal authorities had been unsuccessful. At the same time it was rumored that, if he did return, he would be arrested as an accessory to the killing of Womack by Frank Mahany. Though Radcliffe had not given up his idea of securing control of the Grand Mesa lakes again, he was not foolish enough to risk his life by returning to Delta County at that time.

When Radcliffe realized that his demand for protection was not going to be fulfilled, he took his case to the British ambassador in Washington, D.C. This, in turn, prompted a request to Secretary of State Hay for action and restitution, the financial loss being placed by Radcliffe at $55,000.

MURDER AND MYSTERY ON GRAND MESA

Had Colorado Governor Orman not ignored two letters sent to him by Secretary of State Hay, the issue might not have created an international mess. Through proper channels, Orman had asked Attorney General Post to investigate the claim and to report the findings back to him. Acting on his recommendation, Governor Orman finally responded that Colorado was not liable, because it was not possible for the state authorities to have prevented the attack on Radcliffe's properties, with the burning being done only two days after the killing of Womack. Radcliffe's grievance, once brought to the attention of the British ambassador, resulted in a formal claim against the United States regarding a British subject, and it was to eventually involve the United States Congress and two presidents—two because of the length of time involved in the diplomacy. Upon review of his claim with his lawyer, Radcliffe increased the amount against the United States to $65,000, adding $10,000 damages for "having to go about in constant fear and in peril of my life."

Governor Orman did request that his attorney general investigate the burning incident so that the guilty parties could be prosecuted, but it seemed that no one could be located who had any knowledge of the burning of the hotel and cabins, or even the burning of the hatchery a month later. The fishing issues created by Radcliffe reached all the way to Denver, and the ill will went with it.

Sheriff Wallace of Mesa County had a long conversation with Governor Orman over a long-distance telephone a few days after the killing. He noted that many people were frustrated over seeing the hundreds of pounds of trout shipped almost daily by stage from the lakes, yet they were turned away from fishing there and couldn't feed their families. Perhaps their real frustration was the fact that they needed a permit to fish, even though they were easily obtained, and that they could not fish with dynamite as "bait" anymore. A couple of well-placed sticks of dynamite could fill a wagon full of fish in no time! Sheriff Wallace also described the aristocratic attitude of Radcliffe, and that people felt he was trying to recreate the same English upper-class lifestyle in pioneer America, and the two attitudes did not mix well.

Governor Orman soon realized that there was not a single sympathizer with Radcliffe among the local citizens, except

CHAPTER 21: No Protection, Says Governor

for his employees, and he reasoned that it would be unwise to antagonize the citizens of Delta County any further by the presence of state troops. The governor was also seeing a conflict in sending state troops to protect a foreign citizen living on federal land, since the Radcliffe property was the only privately owned parcel inside the Battlement Mesa Forest Reserve. Governor Orman knew that neither Sheriff Wallace of Mesa County nor Sheriff Smith of Delta County had made a request for state aid. So, the governor decided against any state assistance to Radcliffe, even though he had asked for it—and probably expected it—based on his stature.

Radcliffe then decided to make his appeal to the British vice-consul in Washington (initially by telegram), on the chance that the British government would intervene and convince the United States government to send federal troops to the mesa to protect him, as he felt he needed to be there to save his fish in the hatchery from perishing. There were still, however, two employees of the fish commission looking after the hatchery, with the permission of the mob that had burned the other buildings. At this time, they still thought the fish hatchery was federal property.

William Radcliffe never saw the Grand Mesa lakes again. His home and treasures had been destroyed, and he knew that his life was in peril should he try to return. But he was not ready to just walk away from everything. Even though he reached out to his own government, it would be seven more years before the matter was fully settled. Out of Radcliffe's final claim of $65,000, the U.S. government compensated him only $25,000.

CHAPTER 22

The Mob Returns to the Mesa

Sam Burwell had been hired by the Colorado Fish and Game people to protect the fish hatcheries following the burning of the other buildings in July. "Protection," in this regard, meant to operate the hatchery and protect the fish culture. He was not a "hired gun." On Sunday, August 17, 1901, Sam Burwell was asleep in a room at the fish hatchery near the burned ruins of the Radcliffe hotel and resort when he was awakened about 3 a.m. by a voice asking him to strike a light, which he did momentarily. As he turned around, he observed that he was covered by four pistols and a rifle—not quite what he expected. The men behind

Radcliffe fish hatchery near the shore of Alexander Lake. Also visible are the hotel and Radcliffe's cabin. Photo probably taken right after the killing of William Womack and then published in the Denver Post.
Photo credit: Denver Public Library, Western History Department

CHAPTER 22: The Mob Returns to the Mesa

the weapons requested the whereabouts of Mr. Wintersteen and Bloomfield, both of whom were Colorado Fish and Game Commission employees on Radcliffe's payroll. Both were in charge of the fish hatchery operation at Alexander Lake.

Upon being informed that neither of the men were in the area, the mob, numbering about 30 armed and masked men, searched the hatchery buildings, then removed some of the contents and set fire to the structures. Sam Burwell was not harmed, though there was one cry for a "rope," upon which Sam coolly informed them that there was enough rope under the bed to hang a dozen men. Burwell was not allowed to even remove his clothes from his cabin on the pretense that "he won't need them." According to Sam, the fire also burned $40 which he had in a pocket of his pants.

Meanwhile, the mob was firing their guns—into the air, fortunately. Sam Burwell was allowed to leave the area, but not before being asked (in typical dime-novel dialogue) to "deliver a message to Messrs. Wintersteen, Bloomfield, Puchert, Radcliffe, or anyone else that ever worked for the son of a bitch to stay off of the hill and if they ever appeared there they would be filled with holes." In addition to that message, Burwell later noted that, "They also sent word by me for Judge King to keep his mouth shut or they would hemp him." This was a reference to A.R. King, Radcliffe's lawyer.

Burwell was forced to leave over the mesa to the north, the road taking him to the town of Mesa and De Beque beyond. Once he was out of Delta County, he was met by some sympathetic citizens of Mesa County and escorted to safety. Apparently, the folks on that side of the mesa felt differently about Radcliffe and his employees than the mob rule displayed to the south. To most of them, Radcliffe's fishing rules meant little, and most had never heard of William A. Womack, anyway.

There was speculation later that the timing of the mob was intended to intercept Samuel Bloomfield, who was enroute from Denver and expected to be on the hill that Sunday in August. Fortunately for Bloomfield, his train arrived late Saturday afternoon, and he decided to remain in Delta overnight before heading for the hatcheries at Alexander Lake. News of the fire reached him before his departure, however, and he realized that his life would be in danger if he proceeded to the area, so he lost no time in arranging his return to Denver by train.

Upon his arrival in Denver, he found a number of telegrams confirming the burning of the hatcheries. One from Wintersteen at Plateau City read: "Hatchery burned at 3 o'clock this morning by masked mob of 30 men. No one was there but Sam Burwell. He is all right."

Bloomfield estimated the financial loss to be about $30,000, as well as the loss of about 5,000,000 fish—probably a bit of an exaggeration, but not by much. At the time of this event, William Radcliffe was not in Denver, but in Washington. It would be a few days before he would be able to consult with his fish people to determine their next course of action.

While in Washington, Radcliffe had applied to the Department of Justice for protection of his hatchery operation and for his personal protection, but he was informed that: "... while the Department was most ready to aid and protect, it was impossible under the United States Constitution for the Federal Government to interfere in the affairs of the sovereign state of Colorado." Thus, another door that might have provided aid was closed.

CHAPTER 23

Mahany Goes to Prison

Frank Mahany had spent an uneasy month in the Gunnison County jail when Sheriff George Smith brought him on the train to Chipeta Switch. Chipeta Switch[32] was practically on the Montrose/Delta County line. The date was Monday, August 12, 1901. The prisoner was taken to the ranch of S.P. Gutshall nearby, in Delta County, where Deputy District Attorney Millard F. Fairlamb, A.R. King, and Justice of the Peace Salkeld L. Fairlamb were waiting. In a matter of minutes, Mahany waived preliminary examination and was bound over to the district court. A.R. King was representing the defense, since he was Radcliffe's Delta County attorney, while Millard Fairlamb was representing the prosecution, which in this case was the state of Colorado. Salkeld Fairlamb, Millard's father, was present as the presiding judge hearing the matter.

The Delta Independent of August 16, 1901, reported on this brief visit by Mahany, stating:

> He was then returned to Montrose where he was kept in jail until Tuesday noon when he was taken back to Gunnison and placed in jail. It is said that he was very much afraid of Delta county soil and well he might be too, for if it had been known in time that he was in the county there might have been a "gatherin."

In 1901, there were only two westbound narrow gauge trains each day: one was a passenger train and the other a freight train. The same was true for eastbound trains, from and to Gunnison. Sheriff Smith, with his prisoner, would have arrived at Chipeta

A page from Sheriff George Smith's diary for August 12, 1901, showing the reimbursable expense for bringing Frank A. Mahany from the Gunnison jail to Delta County for his preliminary hearing. The fare was $5.00 each way.
Credit: Art & Gwen (a descendant of George Smith) Cannon

CHAPTER 23: Mahany Goes to Prison

Switch at or near the scheduled time of 2:07 p.m. (freight) or 2:23 p.m. (passenger). Unfortunately, the eastbound trains were scheduled at 11:35 a.m. (freight) and 12:05 p.m. (passenger). Thus, there was no return train to Gunnison following the hearing until the next day.

Though the 12-mile trip to Montrose by wagon or buggy was without incident, Mahany, no doubt, was quite uneasy, as was his escort. Mahany was still very much afraid of Delta County soil, and he was likely very relieved to be back in the Gunnison jail.

Even there, Frank Mahany was still fearful that a mob would take him from his cell and administer their form of justice. It was an action that had been discussed earlier by the Delta mob, but the sheer logistics of getting there in secret was enough to discourage the idea, though the younger hotheads were still in favor of it. According to Gunnison's Sheriff Watson, "strangers" had been observed keeping tabs on the sheriff and his deputies, and he felt the need to be on constant alert. He was prepared to leave at any time for other parts of the state, if necessary, to guarantee the safety of Mahany.

Railroad pass for Delta County Sheriff George Smith, issued in 1901 by the D&RG Railroad. The sheriff could travel free when on official business, however, fares were required for prisoners of the sheriff.
Credit: Art & Gwen (a descendant of George Smith) Cannon

MURDER AND MYSTERY ON GRAND MESA

Mahany's trial took place in Gunnison, Colorado, scheduled there due to a change-of-venue hearing in early September 1901. A Delta trial would have been suicide, and everyone knew it. The state was represented by S.G. McMullin of Grand Junction, prosecuting attorney, assisted by Hon. C. Meade Hammond,[33] a lawyer from Paonia, and D.T. Sapp of Gunnison. The defense was represented by Thomas C. Brown of Gunnison and S.D. Crump of Cripple Creek, Colorado. Even though A.R. King of Delta was Radcliffe's attorney and could have represented Mahany, an out-of-town lawyer was considered for the public trial, primarily for King's safety. At that time, even a friend of Mahany was at risk.

The trial of Frank Mahany started on September 20, 1901. He had been charged with killing William A. Womack and shooting and wounding Frank Hinchman. The evidence submitted in the case was substantially the same as given at the coroner's inquest, with a few exceptions. Mahany testified on his own behalf and stated that he had noticed the butt of a handgun peeking out from a coat tied behind Womack's saddle, and thought that Womack was reaching for the gun when he dismounted at the dam. He went on to say that he stepped to one side so as to get an unobstructed view of Womack so as to be able to shoot him. This was the substance of his original statement of self-defense. There did not appear to be any testimony to prove Mahany's allegation that Womack was armed, excepting for his fishing pole.

Mahany insisted that the killing occurred in self-defense and while he was discharging his duties as deputy game warden. He claimed that parties had threatened his life for two years past, and he believed Womack was one of them. He further stated that he had ordered them away from one lake and they had said he would have to have a warrant to arrest them. Fearing trouble, he sent Wintersteen, another deputy, to make the arrest. The man went to Deep Ward Lake first, and then to the Mahany camp at Island Lake, where the shooting took place. Mahany would not state what caused the shooting or give the words that passed between him and Womack's party, but he insisted that his act was in self-defense. Even Mahany's wife testified that she was nearby and heard the words exchanged between the Womack party and her husband—in effect, corroborating the testimony of her husband.

CHAPTER 23: Mahany Goes to Prison

Deputy Game Warden Wintersteen testified that he did not see the shooting but rode to the site immediately afterward, and was with Womack before he died. When Wintersteen asked Womack why he went to Island Lake, Womack replied that he did not think Mahany would shoot anyone, and that he (Womack) did not know that Mahany did not have to have a warrant to arrest him.

There wasn't any testimony, either at the coroner's inquest months earlier or at the trial, that Mahany had made any statement that Womack or any of his party was under arrest. Other than Mahany's self-defense claim, there was no other evidence introduced that would support the shooting of Womack or any provocation for it.

When the case went to jury on September 21, the prevailing opinion was that the case would result in a hung jury. Because of the late hour on a Saturday night, Judge Stevens deferred hearing the jury verdict until the following Monday.

When the jury filed into the courtroom, the verdict rendered was manslaughter. According to the state law at the time, this was equivalent to no verdict at all, as it should have been "voluntary" or "involuntary" manslaughter. Judge Stevens decided the verdict insufficient and declared that the case would be retried at the next term of the court. Mahany had to wait even longer to know the outcome of the trial.

It was assumed that the error in the verdict was caused by the foreman of the jury neglecting to write the words "voluntary" or "involuntary" before the word "manslaughter" in the jury blank. Following the verdict, it was not clear just what the prosecutors in the case could or would do, or why the verdict was not objected to by the prosecuting attorneys.

On September 27, 1901, Mahany's lawyers waived the filing of a motion for a new trial and stated to the court in Gunnison that Mahany had consented that judgment for involuntary manslaughter be entered on the verdict. The court, however, declined to pass sentence, ordered that the verdict be set aside, and set a date for a new trial, all over the objections of his lawyers.

Mahany had a second trial as a result of this unusual verdict, and the second trial resulted in a verdict of voluntary manslaughter on April 26, 1902. "We, the jury, in the above entitled cause do find the defendant guilty of voluntary manslaughter." It's no wonder that Mahany's lawyers would have been willing to offer a verdict of involuntary manslaughter. In a new trial, they knew the strong likelihood of a voluntary manslaughter verdict.

Following the verdict of voluntary manslaughter, the court passed sentence on Mahany, which read as follows:

> *Therefore it is ordered and adjudged by the Court that the said defendant, Frank A. Mahany be taken from the bar of this Court to the common jail of Gunnison County from whence he came, and from thence by the Sheriff of said Gunnison County within five days from this date, to the penitentiary of this state at Cañon City and be delivered to the Warden or Keeper of said penitentiary and said Warden and Keeper is required and commanded to take the body of the said defendant Frank A. Mahany and him confine in said penitentiary in safe and secure custody for and during the term of not less than six and not more than eight years from and after delivery of the said Frank A. Mahany at the State Penitentiary at*

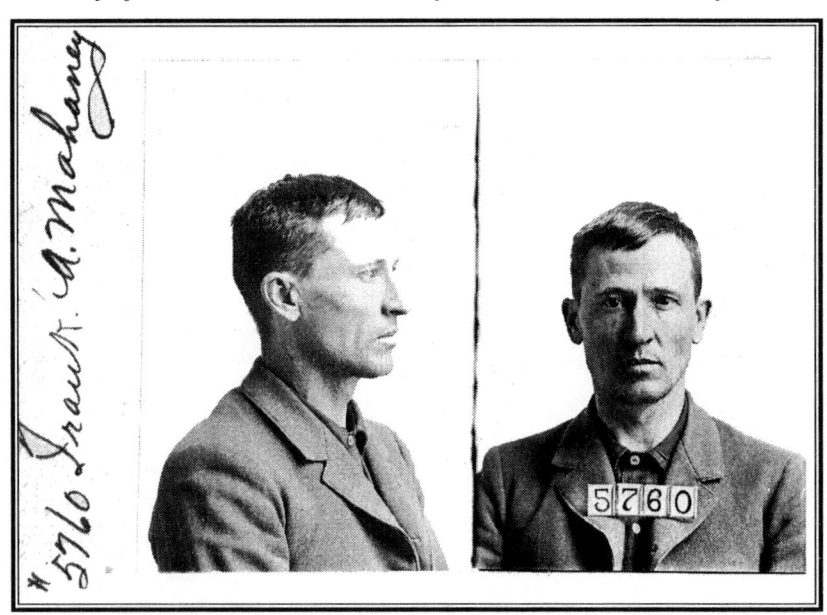

Frank A. Mahany prison photo.

Photo credit: Colorado State Archive

CHAPTER 23: Mahany Goes to Prison

hard labor, and that he be thereafter discharged, and that said defendant pay the costs of this prosecution to be taxed and that execution issue therefor.

Mahany's defense lawyer appealed the verdict to the Colorado Supreme Court, which took over a year and included several other court actions by his attorneys, but the Court upheld the verdict and sentence of the lower court. Frank Mahany was finally transferred to the Colorado State Penitentiary on June 27, 1903. He had been in the Gunnison jail for almost two years. At the Colorado State Penitentiary in Cañon City, he became prisoner #5760.

CHAPTER 24
Radcliffe Returns to Delta

William Radcliffe made no attempt to return to his ranch on Grand Mesa until several months after the Womack killing and the burning of his buildings. In Radcliffe's own words, he wrote, in two separate statements to the British Embassy in Washington, D.C., dated December 20, 1901, that: "On my attempting to return in the month of November last, I was warned by many reputable citizens of Delta County that my life was not worth twenty-four hours purchase; indeed I was met by my counsel at the station before Delta and taken off the train." In the second statement, he wrote: "In the first week of November, 1901, I set out for Delta to consult my attorney there. On his advice and on the advice of other responsible citizens of Delta County, I was stopped at the railway station before Delta, because in their judgment my life in Delta County was not worth a day's purchase, as I would be ambushed and shot from behind a tree within twenty-four hours of my arrival."

The counsel Radcliffe referred to was Alfred R. King of Delta, and it was likely that Radcliffe had initiated the meeting with King by telegram. Radcliffe must have known that his return to Delta County soil would be risky, but he may have thought that the situation had cooled enough for the danger to his life to be minimal. Based on his statements to the British Embassy, it appeared as though Radcliffe had planned to go all the way to Delta. Travelers from and to Denver almost always went by way of the southern route, and this meant Radcliffe would be on the D&RG narrow gauge out of Salida.

It is possible that both Radcliffe and King intended this visit to be secret and, hopefully out of sight of anyone that would rec-

CHAPTER 24: Radcliffe Returns to Delta

ognize the Englishman. To minimize the risk, King traveled to Olathe to remove Radcliffe from the train there, before familiar eyes in Delta knew he was in the area.

Some written accounts of this meeting placed the intercept of Radcliffe at the Montrose, Colorado, station. However, the last stop before Delta was not Montrose, but Chipeta Switch. There were actually three stops between Montrose and Delta—Menoken, Olathe, and Chipeta. Only Olathe was a regular train depot stop.

With Radcliffe off the train, another problem was created. Because of the train schedules, there was no return train east until the following day, the same problem Frank Mahany had only two-and-a-half months earlier when he was brought to Delta County for his preliminary hearing. This time, however, an overnight stay in the Montrose jail was not an option. Radcliffe was essentially stranded in unfriendly territory, being only 10 miles from Delta and lots of rope. But his situation was

A letter written by William Radcliffe to Sheriff George Smith expressing sympathy upon the unexpected death of Smith's wife, Sadie, on August 16, 1899.
Credit: Art & Gwen (a descendant of George Smith) Cannon

certainly anticipated by King. Radcliffe would have known that he would have to remain overnight somewhere in order to catch the eastbound train the following day, and King had only two options left: to bring Radcliffe home with him to "Garnethurst," the name he had attached to his home, and possibly risk discovery, or to take him to Montrose for a secluded meeting there, staying overnight in a local hotel.

Radcliffe had stayed at Garnethurst before, as King's daughter, Ula, was to relate years later. She was 11 at the time. The danger, however, was that even though King's home was an elegant two-story home befitting a successful attorney, it stood like a sentry on a block almost by itself, a serious security issue for Radcliffe's protection.

In her book, *Pioneer Lawyer,* Ula (King) Fairfield mentioned that Radcliffe was pulled off the train in Montrose, but I think she got her story wrong. I believe Radcliffe was put *on* the train in Montrose for his return to Denver.

In truth, the historically accurate scenario isn't that important. What is historically important is that Radcliffe did return to Delta County, or just south of the Delta County line, for a meeting with Alfred King, his Delta County attorney, and he made it back to the safety of Denver, alive.

CHAPTER 25

Radcliffe Sues for Damages

During the morning of July 17, 1901, Radcliffe's employees were forced to leave the resort property under duress, as a mob set about burning the buildings. L.L. Wintersteen, a United States fish culturist and Deputy Game Warden, who was present under arrangement with Radcliffe and the United States Fish and Game Commission, with wardens Puchert and Ball, were grateful that the hatchery operation was untouched, at least at that time. Radcliffe described the destroyed buildings as follows:

- A two-story hotel consisting of nine bedrooms, kitchen, hall, dining and sitting rooms.
- Radcliffe's private dwelling.
- Two other dwelling houses (cabins).
- Two outhouses.
- Stable and barn capable of holding 12 horses and 10 tons of hay, and corral.

There were other buildings and property on his land, consisting of two fish hatcheries, two cabins, an ice house, fencing, piping, cisterns, and other miscellaneous items. These were not destroyed on the night of July 16-17, as the mob apparently believed that they belonged to the United States government. However, a month later—on August 17—it was learned by the mob leaders that these buildings, too, were owned by Radcliffe, and some of the same mob that had acted a month earlier returned to the mesa and burned those buildings, as well.

Radcliffe claimed his monetary damages as follows:

1. Loss and total destruction of his property: $ 4,500
2. Loss by death of the young fish and eggs: $ 4,000
3. Loss from fish taken for two months from his lakes: $ 7,000
4. Loss of possession and loss of goodwill with U.S. Fish and Game Commission and loss of business for years to come: $40,000
5. Damage through having to go about in fear and peril of his life: $10,000

Total $65,000[34]

This claim was presented by the British ambassador to the United States to the Hon. John Hay, Secretary of State, on December 28, 1901, who subsequently forwarded it to the governor of Colorado, who then referred it to his attorney general for investigation. The whole affair was stalled when it was thought that Radcliffe had, at one time, voted in the state of Colorado. Subsequent investigation revealed that Radcliffe had, in 1897, declared his intention to become a United States citizen. No final naturalization papers were ever issued, however, and consequently, though he declared his intention to do so, he never renounced his allegiance to the British Crown. Having filed papers declaring his intention to become a United States citizen, the law at the time actually did permit him to vote, but he never did.

Between December 20, 1901, and March 25, 1904, no fewer than 45 papers/letters/telegrams passed back and forth between the U.S. Secretary of State, British ambassador, governor of Colorado, U.S. attorney general, and British charge d'affaires, in an attempt to resolve the payment for damages listed by William Radcliffe and incurred by a mob following the murder of William A. Womack on July 14, 1901. Public sentiment, speculation, and opinion appeared in a number of media publications during this period of official correspondence, accomplishing nothing more than to keep the issue in front of the public, as it was no doubt a popular item of discussion in local saloons.

The Delta Independent of Friday, May 29, 1903, quoted an article that appeared earlier in the *Denver Times* under the headline: RADCLIFFE WANTS DAMAGES. It read:

CHAPTER 25: Radcliffe Sues for Damages

Governor Peabody received a letter last week from Secretary of State John Hay saying that Hon. S. Michael Herbert, the English ambassador to the United States, has demanded an accounting from Colorado for the destruction of the property of William Radcliffe at Grand Mesa lakes nearly two years ago. It is evident from the tone of the letter that the government of Great Britain wants an immediate settlement and that Secretary Hay is anxious that Colorado should take immediate action in the matter.

For several years Mr. Radcliffe raised spawn for the state on his property at Grand Mesa lakes in Delta county. He claimed the sole use of the lakes and would allow no one to fish on his property. Two years ago this summer one of his employees attempted to drive some fishermen away and in doing so killed one of them. This aroused the anger of the citizens in that vicinity and others whom Radcliffe had refused the right to fish are said to have destroyed his houses and fish hatcheries. The feeling against Radcliffe ran high and he left the state. An appeal was made by him to the United States government, but nothing came of it. After waiting several months he laid the case before the government of Great Britain, of which country he is still a subject, it is claimed. The matter was taken up by Ambassador Herbert and so accounting has been demanded of the state.

Governor Peabody has written District Attorney S.G. McMullin, of Grand Junction, to report on the affair.

At about the same time, another article in *The Delta Independent*, this time quoting an article that had appeared in *The Denver Republican*, reflected the sentiment and opinion of many outside of Delta County. It read:

RESPONSIBILITY IN THE RADCLIFFE AFFAIR

William Radcliffe, the Englishman, whose property was destroyed at Grand Mesa lakes in this state should be reimbursed by the county, if it is responsible, but in no event should his claim for damages be paid by the national government. The national government is not responsible and the people of Colorado do not want it by paying this claim to declare that their state is a dishonest and irresponsible member of the union.

Whether Radcliffe's claim is valid or not is a matter concerning which we are not prepared to express an opinion; but it is clear in any event that the responsibility does not rest upon New York, Massachusetts and the other members of the union apart from Colorado. If congress makes an appropriation for its payment, it will be the same as taking money contributed by the people of the other states along with those of Colorado.

The treaty with Great Britain does not provide that the United States must pay every claim that may be presented against it by a British subject, regardless of whether it is just or unjust. If the claim is not well founded, then it should not be paid by any one. If, however, it is just, the county of Delta or the men who destroyed the property should pay it.

Gov. Peabody has looked into the matter and says that the state is not responsible. Whether this conclusion is correct or not we do not know; but if the facts show that Colorado is under no obligation to reimburse Mr. Radcliffe, unquestionably the same facts show that the national government is under no obligation to pay him. The courts of this state are open. Let him come here and show what ground he has upon which to demand compensation.

Its payment by the national government would be equivalent to a declaration that in the opinion of congress the people of Colorado are hopelessly irresponsible and that, unjust though it may be, the national government will have to shoulder their obligation. As well might the national government assume responsibility for any other state obligation. If it should pay damages in a case like this, why should it not pay bonds and other securities which a state may repudiate. The principal involved should be regarded, and at least congress should make diligent inquiry into the facts before adopting a course which would reflect upon the honor of the people of Colorado. If they are refusing to pay a just obligation then let that fact be established by evidence. It should not be taken for granted without proper inquiry. Denver Republican.

CHAPTER 25: Radcliffe Sues for Damages

The mob rule following the murder of William A. Womack was not ignored by local, state, or federal law enforcement agencies. Even a year after the arson events, the United States Attorney General stated, "Warrants were issued for the arrest of the persons guilty of this lawlessness, and strenuous efforts have been made to apprehend and arrest them, but the Sheriff of Delta County has been, and still is, unable to find them; all efforts for the arrest of said persons have been made by the authorities of Delta County which they in reason could make, but without success."

This was another way of saying that there was no chance that anyone would ever be prosecuted in Delta County for the arson of Radcliffe's buildings. It was no secret that even Sheriff George Smith was sympathetic to the mob action, and he was not about to go out of his way to apprehend any of them, even though he may have known who a few were. He probably still remembered the bullets aimed his way when he approached the mob the night they burned the Radcliffe buildings.

The Department of Justice was asked to investigate Radcliffe's claim for monetary damages, so on February 21, 1903, a special agent of the department was appointed to investigate in Delta. He was Simon G. Kleyn of Holland, Michigan, and his job was to go to Delta County, Colorado, undercover to investigate the killing of William Womack and the subsequent destruction of the fish hatchery and other buildings of William Radcliffe. The murder of Womack had already been dealt with in the courts, but the compensation demanded by Radcliffe for the destruction of his property had not been resolved.

His first action was to visit William Radcliffe in March 1903, then apparently back in New York City, and obtain as much information as possible from him. Kleyn arrived in Denver on April 15 and immediately traveled to Greeley to meet with people in the agricultural community, as his cover was that he was in the beet sugar business and was investigating Delta County as a potential location for a factory to process sugar beets. He arrived in Grand Junction on April 23, visited the beet sugar plant where he obtained literature and correspondence from beet growers, and finally traveled to Delta at the end of the month. He spent May and part of June in Delta "getting acquainted," and it did not take him long to determine that the feelings against Radcliffe were still quite bitter, causing him to exercise extreme caution in any conversation on the subject.

About June 15, Kleyn decided it was time to move closer to the mesa, and he went on to Cedaredge to continue his investigation, reporting, "While the town contains a few good people, a great part are floaters or adventurers, who became squatters and claim jumpers, without regular occupation, and some good ranchmen." Kleyn spent the next three months in Cedaredge. While there, he learned that Henry Kohler, a ranchman; Joseph Hogref, Cedaredge postmaster; Joseph Dale, a ranchman; and Mason M. Colby, also a local ranchman, had all made speeches urging peaceful action the night the first mob gathered to burn Radcliffe's buildings. It seemed to give him some relief that there were a few community leaders who had urged restraint, even though there were louder voices that seemed to prevail at the time.

Based on many conversations he had with local citizens in the area, Kleyn claimed he was even able to obtain the identification of a number of the mob who had been involved in the arson, though even he realized the futility of attempting to prosecute anyone, for no impartial jury could yet be empanelled in Delta County. In his report, Kleyn actually identified, with certainty, several of the mob who had burned the hatchery, and they included Otto Peterson, Jr. and Sr., Frank (wounded by Mahany) and Albert Hinchman, Jefferson B. Reed, several of the Womack brothers, and a number of others. Kleyn also noted that the hatchery arson mob only consisted of 12 to 15 men, hardly the number reported by the press.

When Special Agent Kleyn finally returned to Washington, D.C., about the end of September 1903, his conclusion regarding Radcliffe's claim was that it was a reasonable figure, though why he needed all of the secrecy during his investigation made little sense, unless it was simply for his own protection. Justifying the loss in dollars seemed rather straightforward and could just as easily be determined by interviews with Richard Forrest, the fish and game people, and other former employees of Radcliffe.

It was also learned that Radcliffe had insured the resort and fish culture operation with the Sun Insurance Company of

CHAPTER 25: Radcliffe Sues for Damages

London, England, for a value of $2,250, for which he paid an annual premium of $51. At that time, the hotel was valued at $900; household, hotel, and kitchen furniture at $300; a log and frame cabin (his residence) at $200; furniture in his cabin at $100; one hatchery at $250; and $500 for the furniture and fixtures in the hatchery, including holding troughs, conduits, and pipes.

Radcliffe sued the United States government for $65,000— damages for the fire, et al. It took about eight years for a bill to finally be introduced in Congress to appropriate the money to settle the claim. In 1902, Radcliffe returned to England—still unpaid. Annoyed, he publicly threatened war between England and the United States, though it was not clear to anyone just how he could provoke a war. President Theodore Roosevelt, aware of the bad publicity, made a personal appeal to Congress to pass the appropriation bill. Finally, in 1904, Congress whittled the amount down to $25,000 and Radcliffe agreed to the settlement. However, it took until President William Taft's administration before a joint bill was submitted for a vote. Titled, "An Act For the Relief of William Radcliffe," the one-paragraph bill read as follows:

> *Be it enacted by the Senate and House of Representatives of the United States of America in Congress assembled, that the sum of twenty-five thousand dollars be, and the same is hereby, appropriated, to pay William Radcliffe, a British subject, for damages caused by destruction of his fish hatchery and property in Delta, Colorado, by a mob in nineteen hundred and one.*
>
> Approved, January 9, 1909

Thus, this chapter of William Radcliffe's life was finally closed.

CHAPTER 26

Radcliffe Settles His Affairs and Goes Home

William Radcliffe must have been terribly discouraged and perhaps somewhat humiliated to finally realize that his dream of creating a fishing and hunting resort, as well as the profitability of propagating and marketing fish, was absolutely and indisputably over. He knew that a return to his Grand Mesa home would be at great risk to his life, and with the resort and his home in ruins, there was little reason to do so. The fish hatchery operation, or what was left of it, was now completely in the hands of the state.

He still had many American friends in Denver and in New York City, both places where he felt comfortable and free of danger. Following his failed effort to obtain the protection of Colorado or federal troops, he saw little purpose in remaining in Colorado and traveled east, spending time in Washington, D.C. when necessary to pursue his legal claim, and otherwise, in New York City with friends. Prior to his departure for England, Radcliffe had another legal issue to resolve: He still owned the Grand Mesa property and needed to deal with that before leaving the area.

William Radcliffe realized that he would never see the Grand Mesa again and, at the same time, was probably under pressure by the U.S. Fish and Game Commission to restore activity at his fish hatchery, as the fingerlings were sorely needed to restock the many lakes under their purview throughout Colorado. Perhaps they suggested to Radcliffe that the easiest way to continue the hatchery operation was to lease everything to the state.

Through his Denver attorney, D.C. Beaman, Radcliffe organized the Grand Mesa Lake and Park Company. As the principal

CHAPTER 26: Radcliffe Settles His Affairs and Goes Home

stockholder, he conveyed his fish rights and property to the company. Then on November 15, 1901, Radcliffe, through his new company, leased the lakes to the Federal Bureau of Fisheries and the U.S. Fish and Game Commission, including the exclusive fishing rights, etc., for the sum of $1, for a period of three years. Since this action occurred within two weeks of Radcliffe's visit with his Delta attorney, Alfred R. King, it suggests that Radcliffe was acting on King's advice.

A number of fishermen who persisted in fishing in the lakes without a permit were indicted and prosecuted by a U.S. attorney. They finally were permitted to go free after promising not to repeat the offense.

The Grand Mesa Resort Company, composed of Delta residents who in the 1890s had acquired the S.L. Cockreham claim, continued to oppose the bureau's fishing restrictions. Finally, about 1911, this resort company purchased the interests of Radcliffe and his associates, still identified as the Grand Mesa Lake and Park Company, receiving title to all of his property and fishing privileges. Soon after this, the resort company incorporated. The original members took out stock in the company and sold it at $50 a share to obtain funds. They tried to sell shares in Montrose, Grand Junction, and other neighboring towns but with little success. The vast majority of shares were sold to Delta County people.

From the money obtained, the Grand Mesa Resort Company improved the fish hatchery, restocked the lakes, and upgraded the road from Cedaredge. This road was further improved by the state highway department in 1923 and 1924.

As soon as the Grand Mesa Resort Company obtained Radcliffe's fishing rights in 1911, the Grand Mesa lakes were opened to the public. The company has kept the lakes stocked throughout the years and has never exercised its rights to sell fish. The Fish and Game Commission are allowed to take all of the eggs and spawn in return for restocking the lakes each year.

Perhaps an article that appeared in *The Delta Independent* on May 17, 1912, sums up best the state of affairs for the Grand Mesa Resort Company as noted at the time:

MURDER AND MYSTERY ON GRAND MESA

ABOUT GRAND MESA RESORT

This company has owned and operated in a small way for many years a summer camping ground on Grand Mesa. The property during that time consisted of 160 acres, including portions of Alexander, Barren and Eggleston lakes, all of which are included in the reservoir system of the Surface Creek Ditch and Reservoir company.

Recently the company has acquired the lands and rights of Judge Beaman, being the rights and property originally owned by Alexander & Forrest, and later by Radcliffe of unhappy memory, so the company now owns a little over 320 acres of land, the only patented land on the mesa in the lake region, the fishing and boating rights, as well as the further rights of state license.

There are over twenty lakes varying in size from a few acres to 150 acres, within a radius of one and one-half miles from the cabins. These lakes and connecting streams are the natural habitat of the mountain trout.

Twenty years ago and more, the pioneer disdained the seventeen-dollar rod and gathered his trout with scoop shovel and gunny sack, regardless of spawning time, number, appetite or capacity. These barbaric lapses are less frequent now and most of our people know and realize that a trout has some rights, more especially the right to be caught fairly. To aid in this work, as well as to partake in the joys and sorrows, the profits and otherwise, the ins and outs, ups and downs incident to the best fishing, best climate, finest scenery, best place on earth, everyone should help the project.

It is believed that if the ownership of the property be distributed among our own people, or at least so much as will keep the control among those most vitally interested, that proper protection will be largely given by the public sentiment, and the necessity for the bold bad man with the shot gun and fish warden star to parade the mountain side and talk sassy, will be obviated. The scoop shovel artist and the maneuver of headgates will gradually come to realize his cussedness, become an owner and play fair.

The proceeds of the sale of stock, a limited amount of which is offered, will be used in making the resort property

CHAPTER 26: Radcliffe Settles His Affairs and Goes Home

what it should be—primarily a resort, and next a matter of profit to stockholders. It is proposed first to do about as follows:

First—Make a road up the mountain side—a permanent affair—and instead of climbing a thousand feet in a mile, to do it gently and joyfully in a little over three miles, which multiplies the scenery by five and makes an entire change in the language used along the way. In brief, an automobile road, and in sections where those things go, we can all go.

Second—Gather the spawn persistently, completely and religiously each year, and restock the lakes and waterways until—well, until time to go slower.

Third—Build a small hotel, sufficient for a beginning, a place in which the fisherman can live like the king he is. A few more cabins as the situation demands, fence in the lands, have pasture, cause to cease the vociferous noise occasioned by lost horses, a little store with fishing tackle, bacon, bait and the other things a fisherman needs.

This is about the first season's work. The next and so on, will be to continue the good work, which will, however, be determined at the annual "town meeting" of stock holders.

The capital stock of the company is $25,000, divided into shares of $50 each. The total cost of the combined property and its privileges has been approximately $15,000. One-half this amount has been paid for by stock of the company at par, thus the company owes upon the whole properties about $7,500. This indebtedness is payable about one fifth each year, and it is to provide funds to meet the earlier payments on this and to make the improvements mentioned that the company offers only so many shares of its stock as will suffice for these immediate needs.

Subscriptions for the stock may be made to the secretary or any director of the company. The shares are $50. If the purchaser desires, he may pay $10 down on each share and $10 on each share on the first day of August and February following, until fully paid. In this way, two years may be had in which to pay for stock. Interest at 6 percent per annum on deferred payments. Payments on stock will be receipted for by *the secretary and stock delivered on final payment. All the privileges of the company will be enjoyed by all subscribers for stock, so long as the payments on stock are met when they mature excepting that no dividends will be paid only to those having no indebtedness on their stock.*

Provision has been made whereby every stockholder will be entitled to the occupancy and sole use of a plot of ground on which he may make any improvement desired (not in conflict with the company's interests), those allotments to be as nearly alike as possible in size and desirability, and held under lease from the company, subject to all sanitary and business restrictions, the yearly rental to be merely a nominal sum.

The company officers are: J.A. Curtis, President; J.C. Gale, vice president; I.M. McMurray, secretary treasurer; H.H. Wolbert, M.R. Welch.

The directors are: J.M. Conklin, S.L. Cockreham, R.S. Kelso, C.E. Wetzel, George Deter, John Walker, Ben S. Gheen, A.C. Remington.

The Grand Mesa Resort Company continues to operate on Grand Mesa and today many citizens of Delta and surrounding counties own or rent cabins within the resort. Radcliffe's Hotel was rebuilt in 1921 as a modern lodging and was appropriately named the Alexander Lodge. Several modifications, a number of owners, and many new cabins have become a part of the Alexander Lodge history, now almost 90 years old. Two things are still certain: The fishing is still incredible and the mosquitoes are still abundant.

CHAPTER 27

Mahany is Pardoned and Kills Again

Even before sentence was passed, Annie Mahany, Frank's wife, worked diligently back in Fruita toward obtaining a pardon for her husband. Along with a group of Mahany's friends, Annie submitted a petition to the parole board on November 18, 1904, stating that Womack had threatened Mahany on numerous occasions, and that he had repeatedly been warned about poaching. The petition carried the names of seven of the jurors who had convicted Mahany, at least 50 local businessmen in Gunnison, and many of the residents of Fruita.

When Agent H.B. Kerr of the Humane Society returned to Denver following a trip to Gunnison and the Western Slope region in 1904, he stated that there seemed to be considerable sentiment in Gunnison toward asking for a pardon for Frank Mahany. It was reported to Agent Kerr that the Gunnison County jury that convicted Mahany would almost unanimously ask for his release, as well as the judge, sheriff, and S.G. McMullin, the district attorney who prosecuted him. Perhaps this was due-in-part to the sympathy of the jury and the others for Mahany's family, since it had not gone unnoticed that Mahany had a wife and four very young children, and they were present in the courtroom during the trial.

On November 20, 1904, Frank Mahany was pardoned by the state board of pardons, having served only three-and-a-half years and only one-and-a-half of that had been at the state penitentiary. Mahany was released from prison immediately following the pardon.

His wife, Annie, and their four children had spent the time during Frank's incarceration in Fruita, Colorado, just west of

Grand Junction. Not only was Annie originally from there, but Frank's Uncle Albert lived there as well.

When Frank was released from prison, he boarded the train in Cañon City and rode to Grand Junction, passing nervously through Delta enroute. Mahany didn't know if there was lingering sentiment over his killing of William Womack three-and-a-half years earlier, but he took no chances, keeping a low profile while stopped in Delta.

Somehow, around October 1906, Mahany was able to land a job in Grand Junction as a night watchman and special police officer at the Grand Junction Union Station train depot, working for the Denver & Rio Grande Western Railroad, but on the payroll of the City of Grand Junction. He had moved his family to Grand Junction, locating a home on Colorado Avenue. His primary responsibility was maintaining order at the depot, and that usually meant keeping hoboes and others from riding the rails without a ticket.

It was not uncommon in those times to find convicted criminals in prison one day and wearing a law enforcement badge the next, or vice versa—the legendary Tom Horn being an example of the latter. In his new job, Frank Mahany carried a .38 caliber pistol and a badge. He was a depot policeman and a deputy sheriff. In his first year on the job, he was reported to have made several important captures while on duty at the depot. In his second year on the job, while trying to perform his duty, he reportedly assaulted a man named John C. Wigginton, a leading citizen of Grand Junction, because he would not produce a ticket when asked by Mahany, though he was just waiting for a train. On this occasion, Mahany was arrested, found guilty of assault, and had to pay a fine. Wigginton, on the other hand, sued the railroad for $10,000 for false arrest. The suit was still pending when Mahany's temper got the best of him, once again.

On the night of October 9, 1907, Mahany killed again.

Wade Johnson, a negro, had recently relocated to Grand Junction from Montrose. He had traveled with a female companion, later identified as Minnie Spencer, and they were staying at the St. Regis, where he worked at the St. Regis bar. On the night of the ninth, Johnson informed his companion that he was

CHAPTER 27: Mahany is Pardoned and Kills Again

going downtown for a while, though it is apparent that he had no intention of returning to her. Witnesses where he worked stated that he had met another negro woman, was infatuated with her, and was following her as she had boarded Train No. 6, which Johnson attempted to board—without a ticket.

Witnesses stated that they saw the negro run toward the second car of No. 6 and had boarded the front of the car, when Mahany jumped on board and pulled him off the train. During an ensuing struggle, Mahany—fearing that the negro had a gun, and noting that the negro was the stronger of the two—pulled his own gun and got off three shots, hitting Johnson with all three. Johnson fell dead between the rails, having taken the three bullets in his head, neck, and heart.

On his body they found a half-empty flask of whisky, a box of cocaine, and some trinkets, but no money. He was also wearing two sets of clothes. Lying about six feet from his body was a .32 caliber pistol, having allegedly been drawn by Johnson just before he was shot. Some thought Mahany had planted the pistol to make the killing look like self-defense.

Immediately after the shooting of Johnson, Mahany turned himself in to Sheriff Schrader, and he was promptly locked up in the Mesa County jail. The next day, a coroner's inquest failed to find sufficient grounds for declaring that Mahany was not justified in killing Wade Johnson, though the jury did not exonerate him either, but simply delivered a non-committal verdict. Upon this verdict, Mahany was released from jail.

The next day, T.P. Langdon, a well-known local colored man who was reportedly a friend of Wade Johnson, swore out a warrant against Frank Mahany, charging him with the malicious and willful murder of Johnson. The warrant was sworn to Deputy District Attorney Fry and was served by Sheriff Schrader, and Mahany was jailed, once again.

Mahany's preliminary hearing was next scheduled to be tried on October 14, but his defense attorney, Thomas C. Brown—the same man who defended him in Gunnison in 1901—was ill and unable to conduct his side of the case, so it was postponed to October 24. Unfortunately, Attorney Thomas C. Brown died a few days before the hearing, so another postponement was declared while Brown's law partner studied the case to conduct the defense. Mahany remained in jail, awaiting his hearing on the warrant for murder.

On October 31, Mahany finally had his day in court in front of Justice Joseph P. Sweney. After all the evidence was heard from a large group of witnesses, it was the general opinion that no new evidence had been heard over that previously heard during the coroner's inquest. Thus it was no surprise when, on November 2, Justice Sweney determined there was insufficient evidence to hold Mahany for trial, and he discharged him from custody and any blame of a criminal nature in connection with the shooting of Wade Johnson. Mahany was free once again.

A few months later, *The Daily Sentinel* of February 14, 1908, reported that Frank Mahany had tendered his resignation to the D&RGW Railroad company and was planning to move to Ogden, Utah.

But, Mahany and his family appeared in the 1910 and 1911 city directory of Salt Lake City, Utah, where, according to the directory, he was employed as a "laborer." However, the 1910 Salt Lake City census indicated he was employed as a "hooker" for the railroad. While the profession described in the 1910 census probably brings a smirk to one's face, and maybe some confusion as well, the term "hooker" used in 1910 did not refer to the world's oldest profession. As it relates to the railroad business, a hooker is an engineer on a shunter, which is a switch engine. Quite a shift—from a railroad deputy sheriff/policeman to a specialized railroad engineer.

While in Salt Lake City in 1911, Annie gave birth to their sixth child, a girl, whom they named Martha Clare Mahany. From here on, Frank Mahany's life becomes somewhat fuzzy. The 1920 census finds his wife, Annie, along with four of the children living in San Francisco, California. Frank does not appear to be living with them. This may support the theory that Frank was killed in Pocatello, Idaho, in a confrontation with another man, though the date is unknown and the event is not supported with any factual evidence. Muriel Marshall, in her book, *Island in the Sky*, describes this fate for Mahany without including any references.

Marshall even describes another killing by Mahany that occurred in Ogden, Utah, while he was working, again, for railroad security there. He supposedly killed a white man for riding

CHAPTER 27: Mahany is Pardoned and Kills Again

a through freight train. It was claimed that the citizens in Ogden somehow put pressure on the railroad to have him relocated, this time to Pocatello, again doing police work at the depot.

Neither the states of Utah or Idaho have any record of a killing by Mahany, nor of his death in either state. On the other hand, Mahany family genealogy appearing on internet resources shows that Frank A. Mahany died in 1944 in the Philippines. Attempts to verify this and secure factual evidence with the descendant who posted the information was not successful.

Thus ended the law enforcement career of former deputy game warden and Colorado prisoner #5760.

CHAPTER 28

The Story Continues

William Radcliffe's Colorado adventure was over. His dream of creating a first-class fish and game resort had gone up in smoke, and his return to Delta County was not possible, as he knew his life would be in jeopardy.

Prior to the killing of William Womack, he had already intended to make significant improvements to the resort. His plans included building another large hotel during the fall of 1901. It was to be unique in that the central structure was to consist of only the offices, dining room, kitchen, and hot water and electric plants. The guest chambers were to be cabins of from one to five rooms, scattered throughout the trees. All were to be connected by telephone, have electric lights and hot and cold water, and be attended to by bell boys, porters, chambermaids, and such services, just as in a regular hotel—at least Radcliffe's idea of a regular hotel. He was even planning daily mail service. At least those were the intentions he described to the press.

However, reality had now set in, and he was ready to get on with his life. He had an established familiarity with New York, and his attraction to the city may have been the result of meeting a lady from there who had been a guest at his hotel on the Grand Mesa. She was later identified as Mrs. Catherine Seymore, and she was a widow. She was also born in Kingston, Jamaica, in 1867, and it is quite possible that she and William Radcliffe were acquainted many years earlier. No other details about her are known.

Radcliffe did not remain in New York very long, returning to his native England on March 22, 1902, to Liverpool on the *SS Lucania*, and returning to New York again in 1903.

CHAPTER 28: The Story Continues

Four years later, an article in *The Delta Independent* appearing on July 6, 1906, announced his marriage to Catherine, and it read:

> RADCLIFFE MARRIED
>
> It will be of interest to Delta County people to learn that William Radcliffe, whose cabins and other paraphernalia on Grand Mesa were burned some years ago, has taken unto himself a wife, a lady he met while in this country. The following clipping is taken from the *Denver Post*:
>
> Colorado friends of William Radcliffe, the wealthy English barrister whose home on his estates in Delta County was burned five years ago because of the shooting of a fisherman trespasser will be interested in the announcement of his marriage to Mrs. Catherine Seymore of New York, whom he met on a hunting trip at his estates, to be celebrated in London on July 4.
>
> The President recently allowed Radcliffe an appropriation of $25,000 for the damage he sustained while owning property on the mesa. Those who were connected with the burning had rather expensive fun at the account of the people. Yet the end has justified the means for Uncle Sam now holds what Radcliffe held as his "estate" and the people seem to be contented with the arrangement.

William Radcliffe, as misguided as he was regarding pioneer America, still loved to visit this country. He and Catherine returned to New York again on February 16, 1910, but on that occasion they traveled on the *SS Nile* from Jamaica, only a four-day trip. The ship manifest indicated that they had also traveled in the United States in 1908, though there is no evidence that they visited Colorado.

On May 10, 1938, William Radcliffe died in Kent, England, at the age of 81. Thus ended a turbulent chapter in Delta's early history, and one which will be remembered for years to come.

Richard Forrest had a very different future in store for him. Following his marriage to Mary Ungerman on April 4, 1895, and the sale of the resort and fish business in 1896, he focused on his Eckert ranch and his new family, and continued his farming endeavors. A son, George Richard Forrest, appeared in 1897, and a daughter, Marguerite, in 1901. After the Womack killing and the ultimate conclusion of the entire aftermath, Forrest actually returned to work at the rebuilt fish hatchery on Grand Mesa, transporting fish and fry for the Fish and Game Commission in Leadville. During early spring and late fall, he maintained watch over the hatchery until winter snows precluded travel there.

In early September 1920, Richard Forrest was haying at his Eckert farm and, by a twist of fate, a steel cable encircled his right foot, the other end being attached to a horse. The horse spooked, lunging and tightening the cable, and it cut off his foot. He survived the accident, however, and lived another 20 years. His wife, Mary, died in 1930, after which he went to live with his daughter, Marguerite, in the Chicago, Illinois, area. Richard Forrest died in the summer of 1940, far from his beloved Colorado, but he had lived and played a major role in Delta County's early history.

William Alexander, the man who originally developed his Fish Lake Resort on Grand Mesa and then disappeared, has remained a mystery and an enigma to this day. However, even after he had disappeared early in this story, he somehow continued to make occasional headlines.

And so ends a story of *Murder and Mystery on Grand Mesa*. As always, when one story ends, another begins. Read on!

CHAPTER 29
A Skeleton is Found

Gottlieb Peter Koppenhafer had purchased a 40-acre parcel just west of the town of Cedaredge on March 9, 1905. Kiser Creek passed through their land, almost dividing it in half.

About a year later, in late February 1906, Mrs. Koppenhafer was looking for hidden hen's nests near her home when she came upon what seemed to be a small crevice between two large rocks. Thinking it to be a very likely place for eggs, she began removing some of the small rock at the opening. She had not removed many rocks when she noticed a smooth, round white rock. As she reached for it and lifted it in her hand to examine it more closely, she realized—to her horror—that it was a human skull. She ran to her house to show her husband, who examined it more closely. Thinking the find of no consequence, he did not mention it for a day or so, then thought better of it and came to Delta to report it to county coroner, Dr. Burgin, a highly respected physician in town. The doctor, asking several friends to accompany him, went immediately to the spot where the skull was found and proceeded to investigate further. As they removed the rest of the rocks, it didn't take long to determine that the skull was part of a complete human skeleton, hidden along with the remains of what were believed to be the bones of a dog.

When the question was raised as to who the bones might have belonged to, the immediate speculation was that the bones were the remains of William Alexander, who had disappeared in 1892. Within days, a coroner's inquest followed the discovery of the skeleton and was conducted over a period of two-and-a-half days. The first session of the inquest was held at Cedaredge on Saturday. Delta County Coroner C.H. Burgin and County

Attorney George Stephan conducted the proceedings. W.M. Gill, Malcolm Peterson, Louis Wilcox, Wm.J. Brower, H.H. Whipple, and Luther W. Rood were selected as jurors.

The evidence heard on the first day was from people who were closely acquainted with William Alexander and had some knowledge regarding his disappearance 14 years earlier. The one fact that induced the county authorities to hold an inquest was that the skull found appeared to have abnormally large incisors in front, almost the size of molars, as well as normal molars in the back. This condition, while very unusual, was significant to the investigation, and witness after witness was repeatedly asked concerning them and whether they looked like those of Alexander as they remembered him. However, there was a decided difference in opinion. No witnesses were entirely sure or positive that the skull before them WAS that of Alexander, but there were witnesses who swore that it WAS NOT. The reason for the latter statement was that Alexander was supposed to have had Dr. Dorsey, a one-time dentist in Delta, extract two molars from his left jaw, while the skeleton or skull showed the missing teeth were from a different location.

One of the most significant reasons to believe that these were the remains of Alexander was the fact that he was known to have what some considered as double molars, one tooth of which had been taken out. Both of these conditions were found to be present with the discovered skull. And besides, some believed that Alexander had a head that was shaped largely the same as the skull's. No evidence of force or gunshot was found on the skull or skeleton, with the exception of the bones of one of the legs, which seemed to be shattered and broken.

A comparison of the teeth of the skull and others showed that the lower incisors (the front teeth), although heavy, were not what one might call abnormally so. Yet the upper jaw showed very heavy incisors—in fact, extraordinary. The shape of the skull was, as neighbors remembered, that of Alexander's, but the chin was pointed instead of flat, and Alexander was remembered as having more of a flat chin.

A few days before Alexander's disappearance, he drove Mrs. W.W. Hart and another lady to Montrose to do some shopping, and during the drive, by buggy, the subject of good teeth was

CHAPTER 29: A Skeleton is Found

discussed. Alexander told the ladies what good teeth he had, and exposed a set of abnormally large incisors as large as the rear molars, and Mrs. Hart noticed that one of them was gone. She thought very little of the incident except the oddity of the man having what she described as double front teeth, until she saw the skull of the skeleton that was found on the Koppenhafer ranch, and she said that the teeth in the skeleton corresponded exactly with those of Alexander, even to the missing tooth.

During the investigation, the relationship that existed between Richard Forrest, the former partner of Alexander, was thoroughly gone into. A difference of testimony was evident in this case, as well. Forrest claimed that at no time were their relations of such a bitter nature that any hard feelings remained, while other witnesses claimed that bad blood was between them continually.

While in Delta, it was learned that Alexander had, indeed, purchased the provisions for the lodge from Jack Gale's grocery, and to the list, he apparently had added several bars of hard water soap. This was considered an odd purchase, because that soap was not used at the lodge on Grand Mesa. Why this would matter is anybody's guess.

It was also learned that Alexander had withdrawn all of the remaining funds in the Delta County Bank account of the resort, the exact amount never disclosed to the public, and he had also secured a loan of about $300 from the bank. In addition, he purchased a new saddle at the Wilson saddle shop. Again, it is not known whether this saddle had previously been ordered or whether this was a purchase from store inventory. Finally, Alexander had borrowed a rifle from Jack Gale following the purchase of groceries from his store. This was somewhat unusual, because Alexander was not known for carrying or using a rifle. And when last seen, Alexander was noticed riding through Delta leading a loaded packhorse.

During the inquest, several additional curious recollections were disclosed. William Alexander had repeatedly told different parties that he intended to leave the ranch and travel to New Mexico, a state he claimed to have formerly lived in, and while he was a resident of Wet Mountain Valley (located in Custer County, Colorado), he had disappeared and no one had heard from him for 10 years. This statement would seem to suggest that someone knew Alexander when he lived there, otherwise, it makes no sense. Several others noted that Alexander was in the habit of saying little about his personal affairs and relations and that he was a man who had little fear of anything.

The finding of the body on the trail on a road that was seldom used in traveling between Delta and the lakes was explained by one witness only, C.D. Johnson, who says that Alexander had told him, on the day he was last seen in Delta, that he was going to take the "short cut" home. This piece of evidence was the only remark that would lead one to believe, should this really be the remains of Alexander, that there was a reason why he should have been found so far from the main traveled road.

The discovery of the wagon and harness that is reported to have been on the Hartland Ditch in north Delta was one of the things that was not brought out clearly by the sworn witnesses. The remains of the dogs—there were said to be parts of three canines—could not be explained by anyone, and one of the dogs had evidently been shot, as bullet holes were found in the jaw bone. It was also disproved, contrary to rumor, that Alexander was in the habit of being accompanied by a dog. It was also noted that Alexander had few enemies, but those that he did have were very bitter. No further explanation appeared to explain this statement. Neither was it shown that any men who might be called under popular suspicion could have been involved in the deed.

During the testimony on Tuesday afternoon, it developed that a man named Ford and a man named Roberts were in partnership in a coal mine claim near the spot where these bones in question were found. At one time, it was reported that Ford had jumped a coal claim of a Mr. Fickes. Sentiment for such actions in those days was somewhat vengeful. Sometime in 1889, Roberts called at the place where Ford was boarding and invited him out, and these men both disappeared and nothing had been heard of them ever again. It was also reported that Ford owned and was continually with dogs. So there is a strong possibility that the skeleton could be explained relating to this incident.

The only evidence of rough treatment of the body was a badly splintered femur or leg bone, which had evidently been broken before the decay of the body. It is unlikely that this could

CHAPTER 29: A Skeleton is Found

have occurred while the body was being covered with stones, though that was only speculation by some. The means of death of the man could not be determined, but might have been either by choking or stabbing, as no bullet holes were found in any of the bones.

On Tuesday, the last day of the inquest, Deputy Sheriff Lovitt of Cedaredge and a few others went to the spot where the skeleton was found for the purpose of procuring the remainder of the bones and looking for more evidence for identification. Nothing in the shape of metal or jewelry was found as a clue. The only thing to show that the body had not been entirely stripped when placed there was a bone button about the size of a vest button, but nothing else. The dirt in the immediate vicinity of the bones was all carefully examined and sifted, but nothing else was found.

Lovitt also recalled that a ranchman living in that area remembered finding a number of brass buttons several years earlier at a spot about 200 yards distant from the place where the bones were discovered. The clothing to which they had been attached apparently had been burned, as bits of charred cloth still clung to them. However, at the time, nothing was thought of it, as no one knew of the gruesome discovery that would come several years later.

Dr. Burgin estimated that the body had been there about 12 years and was that of a man between the ages of 30 and 40 years, which certainly did not rule out Alexander.

Dr. Braisted, another Delta physician, methodically measured the bones of the skeleton and, by making allowances for joints, he was convinced that it was that of a man who stood about 5 feet 1 inch tall. He knew Alexander to be a man about 5 feet 6 to 8 inches tall.

Much speculation remained as to how, if these were Alexander's remains, he had traveled so far from his wagon. Older citizens said that there were rumors as to his leaving the country (Colorado) along about the time he came down for the last time. He may have drawn his money from the bank, gone back to his wagon, and suddenly forgotten something that he left on the mesa. Naturally, he would have taken both horses and, inasmuch as he had purchased a new saddle that day, would have chosen to ride back instead of driving. And the spot where the skeleton was found, near Kiser Creek, was not too far from the direct trail to the lakes.

A gunshot in those days was no uncommon thing and would not have been noticed, even had there been those about to hear. But in 1893, there were two outfits on Tongue Creek—one owned a ranch on the south side of the spot where the remains were found and the other was a party of horse breakers who lived above. It may be that these horse breakers knew of the fact that Alexander had drawn a considerable sum of money that day and, taking for granted the supposition that he was traveling back to the lakes is true, waylaid him as he passed along the trail.

The jury finally returned its verdict on Tuesday: "An unknown man was killed and concealed by an unknown party or parties." Circumstantial evidence of 14 years' standing was apt to be very inconclusive, especially when the skeleton was the only physical evidence.

The Delta Independent of March 6, 1906, had this notice under the local news section: "The skull of the man whom so many suppose was William Alexander, can be seen on exhibition in the window of the Independent. Take a glimpse of it if your nerves are strong. Otherwise, look the other way when you pass by." Even then, such oddities were used to sell or draw attention to the local newspapers.

The competing newspaper in Delta, *The Delta County Laborer*,[35] took a more humorous approach to the bones, having just reported on the recent municipal election in Delta, by stating: "It is said that the bones being displayed in the window of the Independent office is all that remains of the once robust Taxpayers party in the town of Delta. Take one last look."

It appears that many did take a last look, and an article in *The Delta Independent* on March 16, 1906, probably ended any speculation regarding this skeleton.

AN INDIAN SKULL
Without Much Doubt the Bones Found Near Cedaredge Those of Aborigine.
During the past few days and since this paper has been exhibiting the skull of the supposed Alexander, many different

CHAPTER 29: A Skeleton is Found

people have had occasion to view the mysterious find. Medical men and dentists have also made close examination and without many doubts there is little now to lead a belief that these are the remains of Alexander.

It has been shown that teeth extracted before death cause a honeycombing of the tissues and after the softer parts of the anatomy have dropped away appear quite solid. As there is no indication of this in the skull in question it remains to be shown that Alexander had all of his teeth before death. And it will be remembered that it was proved that he did not have. Again the color of the bone in the skull found is such to lead many who have dug Indian bones to say that this is apparently the remains of one of that race. The doctors also say that these bones may have been even forty or fifty years old. Again the teeth show very severe usage and it is now claimed that they are not double teeth but simply teeth worn down. The size of the skull today is not over a six or a six and one-eighth. No one has yet said what size hat Alexander required.

Several communications have been received by local parties in regard to the finding, most of them claiming to be relations. Probably the requests for more information have been accentuated by the apparent possibility of a legacy, some of the Denver papers claiming that Alexander was worth a good deal of money while as a matter of fact he was a poor man.

William Alexander was never seen in Delta County again, and his disappearance has been considered a mystery for well over 100 years, in spite of occasional clues following the skeleton incident, which might eventually solve this historical mystery.

Just a few days after the verdict of the coroner's inquest, the editor of *The Delta Independent* sent a letter of inquiry to the mayor of Springer, New Mexico, explaining the circumstances of William Alexander's disappearance and the finding of a skeleton believed to be his remains a few weeks earlier. The basis of the inquiry was to ask if Alexander was known in that area, either currently or in the past. The mayor subsequently asked the *Colfax County Stockman*, a paper published at Springer, to print the following article. It appeared, verbatim, in the March 16, 1906, issue of the *Colfax County Stockman*, as follows:

MURDER AND MYSTERY ON GRAND MESA

SKELETON FOUND

Does anyone in Colfax county know William Alexander, or has known such a man living in this county since 1892? He was supposed to have come here that year from Delta, Colorado, and the discovery of a skeleton near Delta has brought out this inquiry from the Colorado authorities. The following letter received this week, is explanatory, and if the hunted man is around or anyone knowing him, will call at the Stockman office, a nasty affair can probably be cleared up:

Delta, Colorado, March 11, 1906
To the Mayor, Springer

Dear Sir: Pardon us for interrupting your busy moments. But a recent discovery of a skeleton here, near Cedaredge, has brought up an old story of the disappearance of one named William Alexander, formerly, we believe, a resident of the section near your city.

William Alexander was a man about five feet eight, pleasant fellow, and fifteen years ago was about forty five to forty eight years old. He was in partnership here with a man named Forrest, jointly owning a ranch on Grand Mesa. About June 27, 1893, Alexander disappeared and nothing has been heard of him since although much speculation has occurred over what became of him. It is thought by some that Forrest killed him and it is the discovery of the skeleton that has revived the old story. Will you endeavor, if not too much trouble, to have your local paper make mention of this fact and see if William Alexander came to Springer or has been there during the past fourteen years. It will quiet a nasty matter here if you can learn something about it. I send you newspaper clipping which will tell you something about the trouble.

If any of those who know or have known William Alexander, will notify this paper, giving particulars when last they saw him or his present or probable present whereabouts, it will be highly appreciated. Colfax County, New Mexico Stockman.

Then on April 6, 1906, *The Delta Independent* printed the following response.

CHAPTER 29: A Skeleton is Found

ALEXANDER WAS IN NEW MEXICO
Stopped With a Man Near Farmington While on His Way South After Leaving Delta County. The Mystery About Cleared.

Because the Delta Independent made an effort to learn of the whereabouts of William Alexander it now seems that the trouble has been rewarded. On March 11th a letter was sent to the Mayor of Springer, N.M. by this paper and a request was made to have same published in the local paper. It was done. Other papers copied it and the Mayor of Delta received the following letter one day last week. It is self explanatory and will probably result in the clearing up of the whole affair.

Black Rock, N.M. March 25, 1906
To the Mayor of Delta, Delta, Colo.
Dear Sir:

As I lived in Delta County, Colorado, at the time William Alexander disappeared from there in 1893 and knew all about the case and since I left that county and came to New Mexico I met a party who used to live in Delta County - a fellow by the name of William or Bill Young - that Young's Creek west of Cedaredge is named after, and as he was acquainted with Alexander and Forrest AND TOLD ME THAT ALEXANDER STOPPED WITH HIM at Farmington on his way south about the time he LEFT DELTA COUNTY. I write to let you know Wm. Young's post-office address is Farmington, San Juan County, N.M.
Yours res. J. Dee

Letters have been written to Mr. Young and the reply will be published in next week's issue. A good many people in Delta County will be obliged to change an opinion pretty soon and a deplorable condition will be cleared up.

Subsequent issues of *The Delta Independent* made no mention of a reply from Wm. Young or any other mention of the event. It was as though the inquiry had never occurred. Either Wm. Young never received any inquiry or he simply chose not to reply. Either way, the initial response does suggest that William

Alexander did, in fact, skip town with no intention of returning to Delta. Then the question arises—where did he go?

It is worth noting a few other facts about Alexander. As previously mentioned, at the "skeleton" coroner's inquest, one person testified that Alexander had once lived in the Wet Mountain Valley, and that he had disappeared from there for about 10 years. The Wet Mountain Valley is in Custer County, Colorado, which includes the two well-known towns of Westcliffe and Silver Cliff. The 1880 census places a William L. Alexander in Silver Cliff, a widower, working as a carpenter. His birth date was listed as "about 1850," making him age 30 at that time, and would have made him about age 42 when he disappeared in 1892. Note that the letter to the mayor of Springer, New Mexico, estimated his age at 45 to 48. On the other hand, William Alexander, in any legal records available in Delta County, Colorado, never used a middle initial. This particular census also indicated his birthplace as Canada. The "disappearance for 10 years" is also unexplained. Is it possible that he disappeared to Delta County? He was only present in Delta County, Colorado, for about six to seven years. Does this imply that he returned to Silver Cliff, Colorado, and if so, when?

In the September 25, 1941, issue of the *Surface Creek Champion*, Gregory Smith of Cedaredge told the story of Alexander's disappearance and added the following:

> *A short time later a fellow who had worked for Forrest and Alexander, came here from New Mexico and said it couldn't be Alexander (referring to the skeleton) as he had seen him in that state. The sheriff of Delta county at that time thought it would be a good idea to lock this fellow up for a while and make him tell when, or where, he had seen Alexander, but the county commissioners didn't want to put the county to any expense, unless they were sure they had a case, so nothing was done about it and he disappeared about as suddenly as he had appeared after the finding of the skeleton. Few people would have believed his story and maybe he was asked, or told, to tell it. He was never seen around here afterwards.*
>
> *Another man took a trip out in the northwest, somewhere in Oregon, to visit Alexander, but few people thought he would find him, and I don't suppose he did.*

CHAPTER 29: A Skeleton is Found

What became of Wm. Alexander will probably always remain a mystery.

Gregory Smith's recollection of the Oregon connection was not quite accurate, as the final chapters will note.

CHAPTER 30

Alexander Found?

When Delta County readers of *The Delta Independent* opened their newspapers on February 20, 1914, they were informed—in a front page article—that a man named William Alexander had killed two miners in Grants Pass, Oregon, on January 13, and was being held for trial in that town.

> *Two frontiersmen were shot dead in their cabin and the officers of that district have taken and are yet holding for trial a man named William Alexander who once resided in this county and for whom two lakes on Grand Mesa were named. The officers now holding the murderer in Oregon recently gained some knowledge of Alexander's former residence in Delta County and a letter was recently written to parties here making inquiries regarding him, and thus have been revived the memories of old times in Delta County of Alexander's mysterious disappearance from this section.*

Who lived in Grants Pass, Oregon, in 1914 who was also living in Delta County at the time of William Alexander's disappearance in 1892? The answer to this question may have been revealed in a subsequent article.

The first article went on to, once again, tell the story of Alexander's disappearance in 1892 and the finding of the skeleton in 1906. But another curious paragraph disclosed heretofor unknown details of the relationship between William Alexander and Richard Forrest. It read as follows:

> *The Surface Creek Ditch and Reservoir company wanted possession of this reservoir project, now assuming realistic pro-*

CHAPTER 30: Alexander Found?

portions, and one day they made a trade of two 99 year fishing privileges in the two lakes now known to be Alexander lakes, with Alexander, who afterwards went to work to make a resort of the premises. Forrest was not consulted as to this trade or new project and he now puts the query: "What in the world did he want with a pleasure resort here nearly a quarter of a century ago. The farmers were all struggling for an existence, struggling to improve their places and had no thought whatever of pleasures and the establishment of resorts for that purpose." But Forrest was the silent partner [in] the original deal, the other fellow had charge of affairs and he, Forrest, was compelled to accept the terms of the deal made by his active partner. And thus passed from their grasp a valuable reservoir project.

Had Richard Forrest forgotten that the primary purpose of the partnership was the fish business, both raising eggs for spawn in the hatchery and selling fish for consumption throughout the state? And had not he, Forrest, financed the building of the hotel on Grand Mesa?

This particular article does not explain how the William Alexander of Grants Pass, Oregon, was linked to the William Alexander who disappeared from Delta in 1892. It is assumed that the name similarity caught the attention of Catherine E. Springer, a resident of Grants Pass, but formerly a resident of Surface Creek, in Cedaredge, Colorado.

This much we have learned from county records and Delta newspapers: Catherine E. Springer moved to the Surface Creek area sometime between 1895 and 1900. Kansas census records for 1880, 1885, and 1895 showed Catherine E. Springer to be living in Phillips County, Kansas, with her family, while the 1900 census placed her living in Cedaredge, Colorado, also confirmed by Delta County property records.[36]

She moved to Grants Pass in August 1906. She was clearly in the Cedaredge area when the murder of William Womack occurred and certainly had heard the story of William Alexander's disappearance in 1892. Though we have no exact proof, it is almost certain that she never viewed Alexander personally or even saw a photo of him. No confirmed photo of Alexander has ever surfaced, and it is unlikely that there ever was one.

MURDER AND MYSTERY ON GRAND MESA

Catherine Springer did not live in Cedaredge at the time that William Alexander was in the area. However, we do know that she visited relatives in this vicinity twice in 1890—once in April and again in late September—both times accompanied by her 10-year-old son, Caleb. Her home at the time was in Phillipsburg, Kansas. My suspicion is that she never actually saw William Alexander, and for this reason: When the William Alexander in Grants Pass, Oregon, was put in jail awaiting his trial, it was reported that Catherine Springer actually visited him to determine if, in fact, he was the same man who had lived in Delta County years earlier. On April 17, 1914, *The Delta Independent* contained the following statement:

> *Word comes from Mrs. C.E. Springer at Grants Pass, Oregon, that she recently visited the Wm. Alexander held there for murder and who was thought to be the same Alexander who resided here several years ago. She states that the man held there has resided in that county for over 20 years and that he cannot be the same man.*

Had she done the math, she would have realized that Alexander had been gone almost 22 years from Delta County (June 1892 to April 1914). Her sole position was based on Alexander's statement and apparently not her identification or recognition of him from years earlier.

Furthermore, Delta County's William Alexander had committed grand larceny—stolen the bank funds of the resort—on the day he disappeared. The last thing he would want to do would be to compound the charges against him in Grants Pass by admitting a Delta County connection, even though murder kind of trumps grand larceny.

To confuse the issue even more, the editor of the *Delta County Tribune* wrote a letter to Sheriff Will C. Smith of Grants Pass, Oregon, when the possible connection between the two Alexanders was made public, and a reply to his letter was printed in the *Tribune* on April 3, 1914. The letter read as follows:

> *Gentlemen:*
>
> *In response to your letter of the 21st inst. relative to one Wm. Alexander whom we are holding on a double murder*

CHAPTER 30: Alexander Found?

charge, I will say that he states that he never was in Colorado. I am sure that he is not the man whom you refer to, as we have had several letters from your sheriff, county attorney, each, also, a woman from Delta called here to see Alexander, and she stated that he was not the man.
   Yours truly,
      WILL C. SMITH, Sheriff

The only "conclusive" evidence identified by the Grants Pass people seems to be based on William Alexander's own statements and not on any other evidence introduced by the Grants Pass officials. It is strange that they all accepted Alexander's word, but they probably had to, lacking anything else.

When the possible Grants Pass connection was disclosed in February 1914, Richard Forrest announced that he would be traveling immediately to Grants Pass personally to view William Alexander there to verify whether he was his former partner. That would certainly answer the question on everyone's lips.

The newspaper actually reported Richard and Mary Forrest's departure by train the same day. Forrest had stated that he expected to be gone several weeks or possibly months, as he anticipated being present for the trial, as well. Nothing but silence resulted from this apparent trip. Careful review of Delta's two newspapers for the following nine months did not even include a mention of Richard Forrest.

So who was *this* William Alexander? For the killing of the two miners, he was convicted and sentenced to the Oregon State Penitentiary for one to 15 years. He entered prison on April 28, 1914, and was paroled exactly five years later, on April 28, 1919. He was reported to have been age 75 when he entered prison. Prison records showed that he was born in Indiana in about 1839. Alexander shows up in Clackamas County, Oregon, for the 1920 census, indicating his age at 80. Oregon Vital Statistics records show this William Alexander died in Portland, Oregon, on June 14, 1927. There was no obituary printed in any Portland newspaper. Curiously, his prison records showed him to be 5 feet, 7¾ inches in height. If you will recall, the findings at the "skeleton" coroner's inquest estimated Alexander's height at 5 feet, 8 inches. In 1892, this William Alexander would have been age 53. Coincidence, or the same person?

No response was ever received from Richard Forrest, or at least was never reported in the Delta newspapers (there were two newspapers at the time). Odd that such an important finding on his part was never reported. Did he ever get to Grants Pass?

It is interesting to make some other comparisons regarding the two Alexanders. During the "skeleton" coroner's inquest in 1906, as previously reported, it was noted that Alexander's age was estimated to be 45 to 48 and his height about 5 feet 8. When Alexander entered prison in 1914, his prison record in Oregon

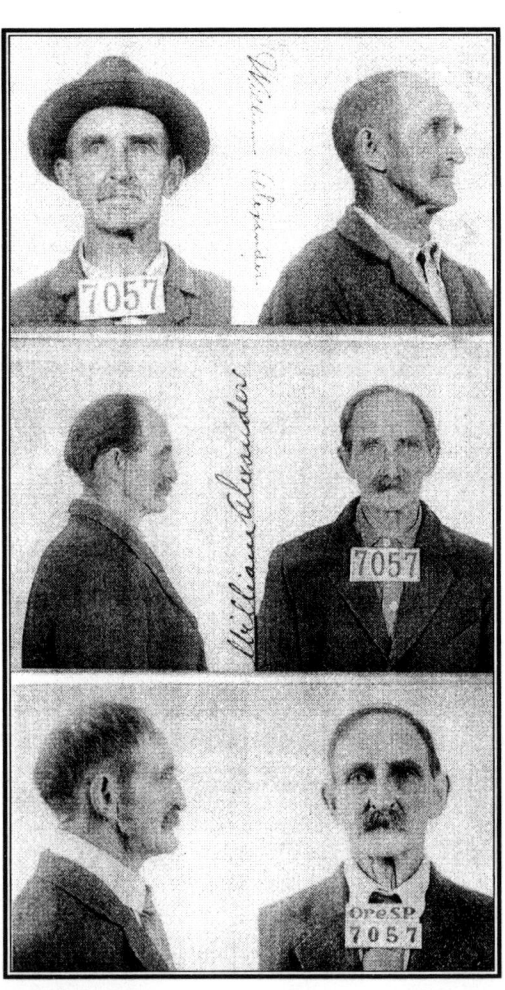

Prison mug shot of William Alexander from the Oregon State Penitentiary, still uncertain whether this is the same William Alexander of Delta County. Photos represent different times during his incarceration.
Credit: Oregon State Archive

CHAPTER 30: Alexander Found?

showed him to be age 75 and his height to be 5 feet 7¾. The Surface Creek Alexander was estimated to have been born about 1844; the Grants Pass Alexander about 1839. The height comparison was within one-fourth inch. Could these two men be the same person?

A few other interesting facts: Oregon prison records showed that William Alexander had been born in Indiana, was single, was a Protestant, a miner by occupation, and could not read or write. Alexander was considered a quiet sort of man, although it was said he was of the kind who wouldn't stand abuse. An article in the Grants Pass newspaper describing the details of the 1914 killing of the two miners made reference to the fact that Alexander's head was injured in a holdup at Crescent City, California, some time back and that may have had something to do with deranging his nervous system. How this was relevant is anybody's guess.

The search for William Alexander was a particular challenge and, aside from the physical facts relating to his disappearance and subsequent travels, what was it that caused him to simply ride off without any notice to anyone?

CHAPTER 31
Author's Comments Regarding William Alexander

My goal in writing this book was to lay out the facts regarding this piece of Colorado's Western Slope history in such a way that the chronology of events made sense, and I chose to do this, first, by clarifying the sequence of events that have been recorded in many publications over the past 100 years or more, and second, by introducing additional information regarding the people and events that would serve to clarify the story, should the reader desire such clarification. I believe I have achieved that goal.

A secondary goal of researching this story was to solve the mystery surrounding the disappearance of William Alexander. While I think I came close to it, I failed to find that one piece of evidence that would leave no doubt about his fate. Ironically, I believe I could make a case for both the "skeleton" Alexander *and* the "Oregon" Alexander as being the Delta County William Alexander of 1890. Let me explain by reviewing both cases and revealing the solid research, as well as the research dead ends.

With regard to the skeleton found in 1906, I felt that the coroner's inquest would answer a lot of questions, but instead, it raised more. The information presented in Chapter 29 was obtained mostly from newspaper accounts of the inquest, not the actual court documents. Those don't seem to exist, or at least they have eluded the Clerk of the (Delta County) Court, the Delta County Coroner, and the Delta County Sheriff, all of whom have access to old county court records within their jurisdiction.

I am bothered by the statement that appeared in only one newspaper article regarding the "withdrawal of the resort bank assets" by William Alexander during his final trip to Delta. It would seem to be a very significant action and, if accurate,

CHAPTER 31: Author's Comments Regarding William Alexander

would certainly lend credence to his purposeful disappearance. The bank in question was the Delta County Bank, which, unfortunately, failed in 1929. Attempts to locate the former ledger records were unsuccessful, even through the Federal Banking Commission. The only other bank in Delta at the time was the Farmers and Merchants Bank, and that ledger book resides at the Delta County Museum. Neither the Alexander-Forrest resort, nor the two men, had an account in that bank.

If Alexander wanted to disappear and was somehow detained and killed by someone, the skeleton found near Kiser Creek could justifiably be his remains. The double teeth could not have been that common, and the fact that Alexander was considered by some to have similar teeth, notwithstanding the few discrepancies among the witnesses, lends strong evidence that the skeleton could have been him. However, the height difference between the skeleton and Alexander would seem to suggest otherwise. Why would the skeleton have been stripped of clothing? Did the killer, not knowing if and when the remains might be discovered, want to hide the identification, and thus support the theory that Alexander had left town on his own accord? If the skeleton was Alexander's remains, why was he killed, and by whom? Was he killed for the new saddle, the money, the groceries?

I can also play the "what if" game regarding Richard Forrest's possible complicity in the killing of his partner. What if Richard Forrest had no knowledge of Alexander's method of acquiring fish back in 1891 when Alexander was caught violating fishing laws, and was incensed at the loss of revenue, not to mention the possible loss of Alexander's ability to repay him money owed? What if Forrest was covering up when he stated in 1914 that the local pioneers were not interested in a resort hotel, as Alexander was promoting, but more interested in feeding their families, even though he (Forrest) had admitted to financing the resort hotel? And finally, why did Forrest claim he was going to Oregon to personally ID the William Alexander there to determine if he was his former partner, and then remain silent about it, almost as though he knew ahead of time that the Oregon Alexander had no link to Delta? In June 1903, Forrest had traveled to southeastern Washington state to look it over to possibly relocate there, and he was there with his family for two-and-a-half months. Did he go back to Washington state, as well? Forrest descendants have correspondence mentioning this trip to Oregon, but there was no comment regarding William Alexander.

Lots of questions and no answers. Was the New Mexico connection a ruse? A check with the Colfax County clerk's office, the custodian of newspaper hardcopies of the *Colfax County Stockman* and another local newspaper of that day revealed that the notice that appeared in *The Delta Independent* in 1906 was, in fact, identical to the notice that appeared in the *Colfax County Stockman* on March 16, 1906, which verifies the statement made in the Delta paper. William Young, formerly a resident of Cedaredge, Colorado, who claimed to have known William Alexander when he lived there, responded that he had seen Alexander in Farmington, New Mexico, "about the time he disappeared."

The finding of the skeleton revived a lot of old memories among the early pioneers, but a span of 14 years had elapsed since Alexander's disappearance, and even the best of memories was bound to experience some "forgotten details." With so much of the Alexander story riding on newspaper writings of the time, it is unfortunate that the accounts of Alexander's disappearance do not exist in either the Delta County Museum microfilm library or in the Colorado Historical Society microfilm archive. In fact, *The Delta Independent* newspapers from late 1891 to August 1893 do not seem to exist in any archive, which, for this research, is unfortunate. In this time frame, *The Delta Independent* was the only Delta County newspaper. There were no others.

I am drawn, once again, to the March 16, 1906, article in *The Delta Independent* that concluded that the skeleton found near Kiser Creek was that of an Indian. Indians were often buried with animals who may have been significant in their lives, such as a dog. We know that when Chief Ouray died in 1880, several of his horses were killed and buried with him. Why not a dog, or several dogs? If this skeleton was 40 or 50 years old, as speculated in that article, then the absence of clothing might suggest that it simply had decayed completely, or that the man was buried without clothing remnants, or that he was lightly clothed to begin with, if an Indian. In 1906, an Indian cultural act such as a burial might not have been widely understood by Delta's pioneer settlers.

CHAPTER 31: Author's Comments Regarding William Alexander

Finally, I draw the reader's attention to the somewhat fuzzy blow-up of the photo of the man sitting on the railing of the Alexander Hotel, taken about 1891, in comparison to the prison mug shot of William Alexander in 1914. Could these two photos be the same person? I will let the reader draw his or her own conclusion. I will end by simply noting that my research is ongoing. Perhaps some other reader of this book will find the missing link to William Alexander, and the final story may take quite a different turn. Stay tuned!

An enlargement of the male person on the second floor balcony as seen in the photo on page 23. It is believed this person might be William Alexander. He is wearing sleeve protectors, suggesting he has some position of importance at the hotel.

Endnotes

1. The Western Slope of Colorado is that portion of the state west of the Continental Divide, which roughly follows the highest parts of the Rocky Mountains.
2. The Preemption Act of 1841 permitted squatters on government land who were heads of households, widows, or single men over 21, who were citizens of the United States or intended to become naturalized, and who had lived there for at least 14 months and improved the land, to purchase up to 160 acres at a price of $1.25 per acre before the land was offered for sale to the public.
3. Stock brand records were researched at the Colorado State Archive and Denver Public Library Western History Department, and no record of the R.A. brand was discovered which might lead to the Colorado county where the brand was first registered. Such information might have provided a valuable clue as to William Alexander's prior residence.
4. Today, we would call this fishing with rod and reel. In Alexander's time, it was referred to as line and hook.
5. The hotel and resort area on Grand Mesa was often referred to in the news media as Mesa Lakes Resort, or Alexander Lakes area. Such writers at the time attached their favorite names to the property, and were not necessarily the names used by Alexander or Forrest.
6. Alexander transported the fish by train from Delta. The fish were probably placed in cans similar to milk cans, in water, covered. In this manner, transport by horse and wagon from the lake to the train depot would have kept the fish fresh. There was no ice house at the time on the mesa.

Endnotes

7. The first fish hatchery in Colorado was built in 1881 about eight miles north of Denver close to the South Platte River. It was called The Denver Hatchery. On the Western Slope, a temporary fish hatchery was completed at Leadville in October 1889, followed by a permanent facility in October 1890.
8. Colorado's first Fish Commissioner was William E. Sisty. He reported directly to the governor. His annual salary was not to exceed $100 and he also was allowed up to $100 for expenses. Sisty served until 1885. In 1881, both salary and expenses were increased to $500.
9. Earthen dams were generally constructed using timber as well as soil.
10. Surface Creek Valley was so named because water flowed year-round in Surface Creek, while other creeks were originally less reliable until reservoirs were created.
11. Twin Lakes is now referred to as "Hotel Twin Reservoir" or "Hotel Twin Lakes."
12. For over 60 years, the Grand Mesa Water Users has controlled irrigation water usage from the Grand Mesa reservoirs that feed creeks and ditches on the south (Delta County) side of the mesa.
13. *Adjudication* is the judicial decree dating a water right. Most of the earliest SCD&RC reservoirs were adjudicated around 1888.
14. In 1901, Sam Cockreham was elected to the office of Delta County Assessor.
15. While Alexander had disappeared at the time this law was enacted, he was still the legal owner, with Forrest, of the resort property.
16. Henning was native to Denmark and had come from a clan of both Olsen and Ungerman surnames. He apparently felt free to use either surname, and sometimes used both.
17. The Delta House survives today as Delta's oldest continuous business using the same name, though it is now an assisted-living residential facility.
18. E.A. Tulian was the Superintendent of the Leadville, Colorado, station of the United States Fish Commission. It was the main Colorado fish hatchery at the time.

19. In just about every publication where Frank Mahany's name was in print, it was spelled incorrectly, typically as Mahaney or Mohoney, though some newspapers even wrote it as McHaney. His family name was Mahany, and that is verified in several documents, including his marriage certificate.
20. The Mahany Building, as it is called today, is still in use in Georgetown, Colorado. Today it is an assisted-living residence with two apartments upstairs and a commercial business at street level.
21. It is an interesting coincidence that County Cork, Ireland, was also the birthplace of Richard Forrest.
22. The Forest Reserve Act of Feb. 24, 1897, stated: "Sec. 1. Any person who shall willfully or maliciously set on fire any timber, underbrush, or grass upon the public domain, or shall carelessly or negligently leave or suffer fire <u>to burn unattended</u> near any timber or other inflammable material, shall be guilty of a misdemeanor, and upon conviction thereof, … shall be fined in a sum not more than five thousand dollars or be imprisoned for a term of not more than two years, or both. Sec. 2. Any person who shall build a camp fire or other fire in, or near any forest, timber, or other inflammable material upon the public domain <u>shall, before leaving said fire, totally extinguish the same</u>." [Underline by author]
23. Cedaredge was then known as "Cedar Edge."
24. Mahany was not lynched, but only because he could not be found by the mob.
25. The lady, as you will note later, was probably an acquaintance whom he married in 1906.
26. The cans were likely similar to milk cans and were used to deliver fish fry to the various lakes for stocking or for transport to Leadville, and were probably also used to transport fish eggs.
27. From the Denver & Rio Grande train schedule of November 1, 1902.
28. From the Colorado Midland Railroad train schedule of June 21, 1901.

Endnotes

29. Osgood's one-car train would have traveled on D&RG rails from Pueblo, west to Salida, then northwest to Leadville, Glenwood Springs, and Carbondale, then from Carbondale to Redstone over the Crystal River Railroad, a standard gauge railway financed by CF&I and completed in 1899. Beyond Redstone, the tracks continued south along the Crystal River to Placita, a total distance of 21.3 miles of rail from Carbondale. The entire length was in operation by late 1900.
30. Cook claimed a Denver paper with the headline "DELTA COUNTY TRAGEDY—DEPUTY GAME WARDEN SHOOTS TO KILL" was handed to Radcliffe. No such headline existed.
31. The Colorado Midland rails did not go through Salida, but out of Leadville they went through Buena Vista, Woodland Park, and down Ute Pass to Colorado Springs, and from there they could go north to Denver or south to Pueblo.
32. The Chipeta Switch was just north of the town of Olathe, Colorado, near the county line. The Gutshall ranch was also located on the Delta County/Montrose County line, within a mile of the railroad.
33. Meade Hammond was a Colorado legislator from Paonia and was the person who sponsored the legislation that led to the Gunnison Tunnel irrigation reclamation project, opened in 1909.
34. This total should be recorded as $65,500, however the total here is reproduced exactly as it appeared in two federal documents relating to the claim of William Radcliffe against the United States. No record has been found that recognized this mathematical error.
35. In August 1902, *The Delta Laborer* became *The Delta County Laborer.*
36. Catherine E. Armentrout married Jacob Springer in 1863, and from that union there were five children. Her husband died in 1899. She lived in Delta County six to seven years before relocating to Oregon in 1906 to live with one of her sons. She remained in Oregon until her death in 1939 at the age of 96.

Bibliography

Books, Journals, and Pamphlets:

Fairfield, Ula King, *Pioneer Lawyer: A Story of the Western Slope of Colorado*, The W.H. Kistler Stationery Co., Denver, Colorado, 1946.

Marshall, Muriel, *Island in the Sky*, Western Reflections, Lake City, Colorado, 1999.

Munsell, F. Darrell, *From Redstone to Ludlow; John Cleveland Osgood's Struggle Against the United Mine Workers of America*, University Press of Colorado, Boulder, Colorado, 2009.

Rockwell, Wilson, *Sunset Slope*, Western Reflections, Ouray, Colorado, 1956.

Shoemaker, Leonard (Len) Calvin, *Saga of a Forest Ranger*, University of Colorado Press, Boulder, Colorado, 1958.

Spurgeon, John M., *Irrigating the Surface Creek Valley*, Lifetime Chronicle Press, Montrose, Colorado, 2007.

The Use of the National Forest Reserves, Regulations and Instructions, Issued by the Secretary of Agriculture, to take effect July 1, 1905, reproduction, 2005.

Wiltzius, William J., *Fish Culture and Stocking in Colorado, 1872-1978*, Colorado Division of Wildlife, June 1885.

Newspapers:

Aspen Democrat, July 3 & 17, 1901, October 12, 1901, Aspen, Colorado.

Basalt Journal, Saturday, July 20, 1901, Basalt, Colorado.

Castle Rock Journal, July 22, 1904, Castle Rock, Colorado.

Colfax County Stockman, March 16, 1906, Springer, New Mexico.

Courier Historical Editor, January 14 and 16, 1914, Grants Pass, Oregon.

Bibliography

Daily Journal, July 18, 1901 and September 6, 1901, Telluride, Colorado.

Delta Chief, various issues, Delta, Colorado.

Delta County Tribune, various issues, Delta, Colorado.

Denver Times, various issues, Denver, Colorado.

Glenwood Post, September 16, 1899, Glenwood Springs, Colorado.

Grand Junction News, July 17, 1901, Grand Junction, Colorado.

Oregon Observer, January 14, 1914 and April 22, 1914, Grants Pass, Oregon.

Plateau Voice, various issues, Collbran, Colorado.

Pueblo Chieftan, Thursday, July 18, 1901, Pueblo, Colorado.

Rocky Mountain News, various issues, Denver, Colorado.

Summit County Journal, September 11, 1920, Breckenridge, Colorado.

Surface Creek Champion, various issues, Cedaredge, Colorado.

The Avalanche Echo, Thursday, July 18, 1901, Glenwood Springs, Colorado.

The Daily News, various issues, Denver, Colorado.

The Daily Sentinel, various issues, Grand Junction, Colorado.

The Delta County Independent, various issues, Delta, Colorado.

The Delta County Laborer, March 6, 1906, Delta, Colorado.

The Delta Independent, various issues, Delta, Colorado.

The Delta Laborer, various issues, Delta, Colorado.

The Denver Post, various issues, Denver, Colorado.

The Denver Republican, various issues, Denver, Colorado.

The Weekly Sentinel, July 27, 1901, Grand Junction, Colorado.

Other:

Grantor & Grantee records, Delta County Clerk & Recorder's office, spanning 1883 to 1912.

Grantor & Grantee records, Mesa County Clerk & Recorder's office, spanning 1883 to 1912.

Grantor & Grantee records, Garfield County Clerk & Recorder's office, spanning 1883 to 1912.

Grantor & Grantee records, Pitkin County Clerk & Recorder's office, spanning 1883 to 1912.

Grantor & Grantee records, Gunnison County Clerk & Recorder's office, spanning 1881 to 1891.

Records of Incorporation, Delta County Clerk & Recorder's office, spanning 1883 to 1900.

Stock Records of the Surface Creek Ditch and Reservoir Company, years 1886 to 1905, Grand Mesa Water Users Office, Cedaredge, Colorado.

Periodicals:
Field & Farm, May 8, 1897, November 23, 1901.

Outdoor Life, January 1903.

The Historian, "Mystery, Murder on Grand Mesa," by Sandra Hopper, February 1995.

Western Sportsman, Vol. 5, No. 3, "Fishing Feud Lasts 50 Years," by Alice Spencer Cook, August 1940.

Western Sportsman, Vol. 5, No. 4, "Fishing Feud Lasts 50 Years," by Alice Spencer Cook, September 1940.

Interviews:
Chaya, Elizabeth, descendant of Richard Forrest, Minnesota.

Jackson, Ethel (Fairlamb), descendant of Millard F. Fairlamb, Delta, Colorado.

Fairlamb, Millard S., descendant of Millard F. Fairlamb, Delta, Colorado.

Index

Alexander, William, 9, 13-17, 20, 21, 29, 31, 33-35, 37, 38, 40, 42, 46, 54, 142-145, 148-152, 154-163
Alexander Hotel, 22, 23, 42, 163
Alexander Lake, 15, 16, 22, 24, 25, 30, 33, 35, 39, 41, 42, 56, 58, 89-91, 111
Alexander Lakes, 25, 36, 44, 50, 56, 58-60, 65, 155
Alexander Lodge, 134
Allen, Sarah Viola, 42

Ball, Edward M., 88-90, 123
Barren Lake, 15, 42
Battlement Mesa Forest Reserve, 40, 72-74, 109
Beaman, David C., 61, 62, 66, 95-98, 101, 130, 132
Bear, H.C., 43
Beaver Dam, 64
Beaver Lake, 64
Bloomfield, Samuel, 66, 111, 112
Botsford, Alfred, 48
Braisted, Dr., 147
Brower, Wm. J., 144
Brown, Annie, 71
Brown, Thomas C., 116, 137
Brunot, Philip, 11
Burgin, Dr. C.H., 143, 147
Burwell, Samuel M., 110-112

Campbell, Charles, 14
Campbell, E.F., 60
Carbondale, Colorado, 94, 95, 98, 101

Carp Lake, 64
Cedaredge, Colorado, 8, 33, 52, 54, 70, 79, 80, 86, 87, 93, 103, 128, 131, 143, 147, 148, 150-152, 155, 156, 162
CF&I, 96, 97
Chipeta Switch, 113, 121
Clackamas County, Oregon, 157
Cockreham, Samuel L., 33, 42-44, 74, 131, 134
Colby, Mason M., 128
Colby Canyon, 48, 49
Cole family, 53
Colfax County Stockman, 149, 162
Colorado Fuel & Iron Company, 62, 95, 96
Colorado Midland Railroad, 94, 95, 98
Colorado Springs, Colorado, 98
Colorado State Penitentiary, 119
Commercial Hotel, 51
Conklin, I.M., 43, 134
Cook, Alice Spencer, 94-96, 99
coroner's inquest, 80, 81, 116, 117, 137, 138, 143, 149, 152, 157, 158, 160
County Cork, Ireland, 18, 71
Crawford, George, 7, 12
Crump, S.D., 116
Crystal River Railroad, 98
Crystal River Ranch, 95
Curtis, J.A., 43, 134
Curtis, O.T., 73
Custer, George Armstrong, 11
Custer County, Colorado, 145, 152

D&RG, 94, 97, 98, 100, 120, 138
D&RGW, 138
Dale, Joseph, 128
De Beque, Colorado, 25, 73, 94, 101, 102, 111
Deep Slough Reservoir, 64
Deep Ward Lake, 75, 77, 78, 116
Delta County Bank, 48, 145, 161
Delta County Museum, 161, 162
Delta House, 45, 54
Denver & Rio Grande Railroad, 45, 94, 98, 136
Denver Club, 48, 50
Deter, George, 134
Dorsey, Dr., 144
Duke, George H., 43
dynamite, 16, 56, 61, 108

Eckert, Colorado, 19, 20, 22, 35, 36, 38, 46, 48, 52, 54, 80, 81, 141, 142
Eggleston Lake, 42

Fairfield, Dr., 80
Fairfield, Ula (King), 122
Fairlamb, Millard F., 84, 113
Fairlamb, Salkeld L., 113
Farmers and Merchants Bank, 161
Federal Bureau of Fisheries, 131
Fish and Game Commission, 17, 51, 61, 86, 89, 105, 107, 111, 123, 130, 131, 142
fish culture, 22, 31, 38-40, 42, 48, 57, 110, 128
fish hatchery, 16, 17, 21, 22, 25, 40, 57, 61, 66, 69, 86, 89-91, 93, 109-111, 127, 129-131, 142
Fish Lake, 15, 16, 38, 142
Fogg, H., 43
Forest Service, 31
Forrest
    Mary, 157

Richard, 13, 18-22, 24-26, 29, 31, 34-36, 38-40, 43-48, 51, 56-58, 60, 65, 128, 132, 141, 142, 145, 150-152, 154, 155, 157, 158, 161
    William, 19
Forrest Hotel, 35
Fort Crawford, 12
Francis, A.T., 51
Fruita, Colorado, 71, 135
Fruitgrowers Reservoir, 20
Fry, District Attorney, 137

Gale, Jack C., 87, 90, 134, 145
Gale Brothers, 22
Game Warden, 58, 72, 78, 79, 86, 99, 117, 123
Garfield County, Colorado, 95
Garnethurst, 122
Getty, H.C., 81
Gheen, Ben S., 43, 134
Gill, W.M., 144
Gipe
    George, 77
    Ray, 77
Glenwood Springs, Colorado, 94-96, 100, 101
Grand Junction, Colorado, 7, 12, 23, 25, 26, 45, 87, 92, 94, 98, 100, 101, 116, 125, 127, 131, 136
Grand Mesa Feud, 8, 31
Grand Mesa Lake and Park Company, 130, 131
Grand Mesa lakes, 40, 52, 55, 61, 65, 92, 105, 107, 109, 125, 131
Grand Mesa Resort Company, 44, 73, 131, 134
Grand Mesa Water Users, 31
Grand Valley, 28
Grants Pass, Oregon, 154-159
Gule, G.C., 43

Index

Gunnison County, Colorado, 11-13, 19, 85, 96, 113, 118, 135
Gunnison County jail, 85, 113
Gutshall, S.P., 113

Hammond, Hon. C. Meade, 116
Harris, Charles W., 72, 99, 100, 103-105, 107
Harrison, President Benjamin, 7, 73
Hart, Mrs., 145
Hart, W.W., 144
Hartland Ditch, 33, 146
Harts Basin, 20, 48
Hay, Secretary of State, 107, 124, 125
Hick, Dr. L.A., 79
Hinchman
   Albert, 128
   Frank, 77-79, 103, 116
Hogref, Joseph, 128
Homestead Act, 12, 40
Horn, Tom, 136
Hotchkiss, Colorado, 42, 89
Houts, S.B., 84

Ignacio, Colorado, 11
Island in the Sky, 138
Island Lake, 75, 78-80, 82, 84, 116, 117

James, Jesse, 18
Johnson, C.D., 146
Johnson, C.J., 43
Johnson, T.H., 64, 66
Johnson, Wade, 136-138

Kellog, R.S., 43
Kelso, R.S., 134
Kennedy, Julian, 96
Kennicott Park, 77
Kerr, H.B., 135
King, Alfred R., 93, 94, 111, 113, 116, 120-122, 131

Kingston, Jamaica, 49, 140, 141
Kiser Creek, 15, 29, 143, 148, 161, 162
Kleyn, Simon G., 127, 128
Kohler, Henry, 128
Koppenhafer, Gottlieb Peter, 143, 145
Kreutzer, William, 72, 73

Lake County, Colorado, 11
Lamar, James R., 82, 84, 87
Land, Commissioner, 24, 25
Langdon, T.P., 137
Leadville, Colorado, 11, 12, 24, 25, 57, 61, 65, 86, 97, 142
Little Bighorn, 11
Lovitt, Sam, 147

Mahany
   Albert, 136
   Annie, 135
   Frank A., 58, 71-79, 81, 82, 84, 85, 93, 97, 103-107, 113, 115-119, 121, 135-139
   Jeremiah, 71
   Martha Clare, 138
   Mary Ethel, 71, 75
   Paul, 71, 75
   Ralph, 71, 75
   Sarah, 71
   Sarah Esther, 71, 75
Mahany Gold Mining Company, 71
Marshall, Muriel, 138
McMullin, S.G., 116, 125, 135
McMurray, I.M., 43, 134
Mears, Otto, 13
Meeker, Nathan C., 11
Meeker Massacre, 12
Menoken, Colorado, 121
Merwin, Attorney General, 106
Mesa County, Colorado, 28, 51, 71, 108, 109, 111, 137

Military Park, 12
Miller, Dr., 79
Milton, Sam, 77, 78
Montrose, Colorado, 11-13, 19, 45, 85, 100, 113, 115, 121, 122, 131, 136, 144
Morgan, J.P., 96
Mower, Clarence, 36

narrow gauge, 19, 45, 94, 100, 113, 120

Ogden, Utah, 138, 139
Olathe, Colorado, 85, 121
Oregon State Penitentiary, 157
Orman, Governor James B., 75, 98, 104-109
Osgood, John C., 95-102
Ouray, Chief, 10, 11, 162
Ouray, Colorado, 19, 24, 85
Owens, Deputy Charles, 84, 85
Oxford University, 49

Peabody, Governor, 125, 126
Peterson, Malcolm, 144
Peterson, Otto C., 52, 128
Pioneer Lawyer, 122
Pitkin County, Colorado, 95, 96
Plateau City, Colorado, 112
Pocatello, Idaho, 138, 139
Post, Attorney General, 92, 96, 108, 141
preemption, 9, 14, 29, 30, 38, 42, 74
Puchert, Henry J., 67, 87-91, 111, 123
Pueblo, Colorado, 96-98, 100

Radcliffe
　Jane (Wilson), 49
　John, 49
　William, 9, 13, 17, 39, 44, 47-52, 56-60, 62-73, 75, 78, 80-82, 85-102, 104-112, 120-132, 134, 140, 141
Radcliffe Hotel, 74, 110
Redstone, Colorado, 94-98, 101, 102
Reed
　Jefferson B., 74, 81, 88, 128
　Leon, 75
Remington, A.C., 134
Rocky Mountain News, 85, 97, 103
Rood, Luther W., 144
Roosevelt, President Theodore, 8, 129

Salt Lake City, Utah, 45, 138
San Francisco, California, 138
Sapp, D.T., 116
SCD&RC, 15, 30-32, 38-40, 48, 51, 65, 74
Schrader, Sheriff, 137
seine, 17, 27, 52, 57
Seymore, Catherine, 140, 141
Sheep Slough, 64
Silver Cliff, Colorado, 152
Simpson, W. Ray, 43
Smith
　Deputy Tom, 84
　Sheriff George, 79, 84, 85, 87, 88, 90, 106, 107, 109, 113, 127
Smith, Gregory, 152, 153
Smith, Jefferson, 93, 98, 101, 102
Smith, Newton, 51
Smith, Will C., 156, 157
Spencer, Minnie, 136
Springer, Catherine E., 155, 156
Springer, New Mexico, 149, 152
SS Lucania, 140
Standish, O.J., 43
Stephan, George, 144
Stroud, Bert, 25
Sun Insurance Company, 128
Supreme Court, 119

Index

Surface Creek Ditch and
  Reservoir Company, 9, 14, 15,
  17, 29-32, 38, 39, 48, 54, 60, 66,
  74, 77, 132, 154
Surface Creek Valley, 14, 19, 28,
  29, 40, 84, 88
Swan, J.S., 59
Sweney, Justice Joseph P., 138

Taft, President William, 129
Teachout, E.C., 42
The Daily Sentinel, 87, 138
The Delta County Laborer, 148
The Delta Independent, 15, 21, 44,
  47, 59, 93, 113, 124, 125, 131,
  141, 148-151, 154, 156, 162
The Delta Laborer, 58, 59, 93
The Denver Republican, 71, 87, 89,
  93-95, 97-101, 125, 126
Tongue Creek, 29, 52, 148
Trickel, Frank L., 77, 79, 80
Tulian, E.A., 65
Twin Lakes, 15, 30, 39

Ungerman, Mary, 45, 141
Union Station, 136
Upper Eggleston, 64
Ute Reservation, 7, 10-12

Walker, John, 134
Wallace, Sheriff, 108, 109
Ward Creek, 29
Washington, D.C., 107, 120, 128
Watson, Sheriff, 115
Weir, Sarah A., 19
Welch, Milton R., 134
Westcliffe, Colorado, 152
Western Slope, 7, 10-12, 19, 45,
  135, 160
Wet Mountain Valley, 145, 152
Wetzel, C.E., 43, 134
Whipple, H.H., 144
Wigginton, John C., 136

Wilcox, Louis, 144
Wilson Saddle Shop, 145
Wintersteen, L.L., 78, 79, 86-90,
  111, 112, 116, 117, 123
Winton Mine, 54
Wolbert, H.H., 43, 134
Womack
  Eliza, 53, 79
  Lydia, 79
  William A., 9, 30-32, 52-55,
  77-82, 84, 86-88, 90-93, 97, 103,
  104, 107, 108, 111, 116, 117,
  120, 124, 127, 135, 136, 140,
  142, 155
Wright, G., 43

Young, William, 162
Young's Creek, 29, 151

About the Author

This book marks Jim Wetzel's second historical book project. He has been an avid Delta County historian for the past thirteen years. As the Director and Curator of Delta's history museum, Wetzel has studied local history at length. His strength lies in his thorough research and attention to detail. He noted early that historical research is often the process of comparing differing historical accounts of an event or story, and then digging out the correct details from yet other resources. His research is meticulous and thorough.

Having lived in Colorado for almost 40 years, Wetzel has the greatest respect for Colorado's early pioneers. He has also studied many of the early western lawmen and outlaws, and occasionally discovers new facts regarding some of those whose paths crossed in Delta County.

Wetzel's interest in and knowledge of early Delta County history turned his attention to the story often referred to as the *Grand Mesa Feud*, and the more he studied the history of the event, the more inconsistencies he noted. The complete story of this murder on Grand Mesa has never been told. It is the characters who bring the story to life, and Wetzel has brought new details of their lives into the story, adding balance and perspective to this piece of Colorado history.